Reconstructing

Paul Bradshaw is Professor of Liturgy at the University of Notre Dame, Indiana, USA, and holds a PhD from London University, a DD from Oxford University, and an honorary DD from the General Theological Seminary, New York. Between 1995 and 2008 he served as Director of Notre Dame's London Undergraduate Program, and still teaches there periodically. He is an honorary Canon of the Episcopal Diocese of Northern Indiana, priest-vicar of Westminster Abbey, and a member of the Church of England Liturgical Commission. He is also one of only two people ever to have been president of both the North American Academy of Liturgy (1993–94) and the international Societas Liturgica (1993–95), and from 1987 to 2005 he was editor-in-chief of the journal, *Studia Liturgica*. Before beginning to teach at Notre Dame in 1985, he was successively Director of Studies at Chichester Theological College, Course Director in the St Albans Diocese Ministerial Training Scheme, and Vice-Principal of Ripon College, Cuddesdon, Oxford.

Dr Bradshaw has written or edited more than twenty books, together with over ninety essays or articles in periodicals. His major publications include *Daily Prayer in the Early Church* (SPCK, 1981; Oxford University Press, 1982; Wipf & Stock, 2008), *The Search for the Origins of Christian Worship* (SPCK/Oxford University Press, 1992, 2nd edn 2002; translated into French and Italian, with Japanese and Russian translations forthcoming), and *Eucharistic Origins* (SPCK/Oxford University Press, 2004).

*This book is dedicated to the one
from whom I constantly learn so much*

RECONSTRUCTING EARLY CHRISTIAN WORSHIP

PAUL F. BRADSHAW

A PUEBLO BOOK

Liturgical Press   Collegeville, Minnesota
www.litpress.org

A Pueblo Book published in 2010 for the United States and Canada by
LITURGICAL PRESS
Collegeville, Minnesota 56321

First published in 2009 by the Society for Promoting Christian Knowledge.

Cover design and photo of marble fragment by David Manahan, OSB.

Unless otherwise noted, English translations of Scripture and other primary
sources are by the author.

1	2	3	4	5	6	7	8	9

ISBN 978-0-8146-6245-8

Contents

Abbreviations

AIR   E. J. Yarnold, *The Awe-Inspiring Rites of Initiation* (St Paul's Publications, Slough 1971; 2nd edn, T & T Clark, Edinburgh/ The Liturgical Press, Collegeville 1994)

DBL   E. C. Whitaker (ed.), *Documents of the Baptismal Liturgy*, revised and expanded by Maxwell E. Johnson (SPCK, London 2003)

ET   English translation

MECL   James W. McKinnon, *Music in Early Christian Literature* (Cambridge University Press, Cambridge 1987)

NPNF   *A Select Library of Nicene and Post-Nicene Fathers*, ed. Philip Schaff and Henry Wace (1893)

Introduction

This book does not pretend to be a complete description of what early Christian worship might have been like. Such a venture would in any case be impossible because of the limitations of our historical information and the caution that modern critical methods place upon what we may assume with regard to the gaps in our knowledge. Instead, it builds upon the approach set out in my *Search for the Origins of Christian Worship* (2nd edn, SPCK, London/Oxford University Press, New York 2002) and attempts to drill down, as it were, at several key points beneath the surface impression that has been accepted in most earlier studies of the primary sources. Its aim has been to see whether a somewhat different picture emerges when one examines that material with altered presuppositions and a more questioning attitude towards it. Thus, each of the chapters begins from the conventional depiction of its topic, and subjects the sources to an assessment from the perspective of the methodology set out in my earlier work, which then leads to new conclusions. This change in our perception not only affects how we reconstruct our vision of the past but also how we use the past as precedent for worship practice today. As an indicator of the effect that it might have on the latter, each chapter ends with a comment, even if in some cases only brief, on the possible modern application of these discoveries.

Many of the chapters are versions or major revisions of material that has been published in other places. Chapter 1, originally given as a public lecture at the University of Notre Dame in 2006, will also appear in Maxwell Johnson (ed.), *Issues in Eucharistic Praying* (The Liturgical Press, Collegeville 2010). Chapter 2 is an adaptation of 'The Reception of Communion in Early Christianity', *Studia Liturgica* 37 (2007), pp. 164–80. Chapter 3 is a new composition that draws in part upon 'Yet Another Explanation of *Didache* 9–10', *Studia Liturgica* 36 (2006), pp. 124–8 and 'Hippolytus Revisited: The Identity of the So-Called "Apostolic Tradition"', *Liturgy* 16 (2000), pp. 7–11. Chapter 4 is a very substantial revision of 'The Gospel and the Catechumenate in the Third Century', *Journal of Theological Studies* 50 (1999), pp. 143–52. Chapter 5 is adapted from 'The Profession of Faith in Early Christian Baptism', published both in *Ecclesia Orans* 23 (2006), pp. 337–55 and in *Evangelical Quarterly* 78 (2006), pp. 101–15. Chapter 6 has been contributed to a forthcoming Festschrift for Bryan Spinks, *The Serious Business of Worship*, edited by

Simon Jones and Melanie Ross (Continuum, London). Chapter 7 is a greatly updated version of 'Cathedral vs Monastery: The Only Alternatives for the Liturgy of the Hours?', in J. Neil Alexander (ed.), *Time and Community: Studies in Liturgical History and Theology* (Pastoral Press, Washington, DC 1990), pp. 123–36. Chapter 8 is lightly revised from 'From Word to Action: The Changing Role of Psalmody in Early Christianity', in Martin Dudley (ed.), *Like a Two-Edged Sword: The Word of God in Liturgy and History* (Canterbury Press, Norwich 1995), pp. 21–37. Chapter 9 recently appeared as 'The Emergence of Penitential Prayer in Early Christianity', in Mark J. Boda, Daniel K. Falk, and Rodney A. Werline (eds), *Seeking the Favor of God*, vol. 3: *The Impact of Penitential Prayer beyond Second Temple Judaism* (Society of Biblical Literature, Atlanta 2008), pp. 185–96 (Copyright © Society of Biblical Literature, used by permission).

PAUL F. BRADSHAW

Part 1
EUCHARIST

1

Did Jesus institute the eucharist at the Last Supper?

The answer to the question posed in my title might seem obvious: 'Of course he did; we have the evidence of the Synoptic Gospels to prove it.' But as you may well have guessed already, I do not think it is as simple as that. Otherwise, this would turn out to be a very short chapter.[1]

The Fourth Gospel

Let us start with St John's Gospel, where there is no account of the institution of the eucharist within the narrative of the Last Supper. Commentators usually say that John has deliberately missed it out and for his own reasons replaced it with the account of Jesus washing the disciples' feet. But that is to assume that the Evangelist – and every Christian of the time – knew that the account of the institution of the eucharist really did belong with the Last Supper, and he chose not to put it there. But that is precisely to beg the question. We do not actually know whether anyone in the first century other than the writers of the Synoptic Gospels and St Paul thought it took place on the night before Jesus died – and even St Paul does not say that occasion was a Passover meal as the others do. So if we suppose for the sake of argument that the writer of the Fourth Gospel did not know of a tradition that Jesus said that bread and wine were his body and blood at the Last Supper, is there anywhere else in that Gospel that might look like an institution narrative?

What about chapter 6? Here we have the account of the feeding of the five thousand by Jesus, in which twelve baskets are filled with the leftovers from five barley loaves. And then, referring back to it on the following day, Jesus says that it was not Moses who gave them the bread from heaven; 'my Father gives you the true bread from heaven. For the bread of God is that which comes down from heaven and gives life to the world' (John

---

[1] Some of the material in this chapter has already appeared in a different form in my book, *Eucharistic Origins* (SPCK, London/Oxford University Press, New York 2004), to which the reader is referred for further details on a number of points.

6.32–3). And he goes on to say, 'I am the bread of life . . . I am the living bread that came down from heaven . . . and the bread that I shall give for the life of the world is my flesh' (John 6.48, 51). Several scholars have already suggested that this latter statement is John's version of the saying over the bread at the Last Supper,[2] and some have claimed that this form could in one way at least be closer to the original, as neither Hebrew nor Aramaic have a word for 'body' as we understand the term, and so what Jesus would have said at the Last Supper would have been the Aramaic equivalent of 'This is my flesh'.[3]

There is, however, a difference of opinion among scholars as to whether what follows (and some would say even verse 51c itself) is an integral part of the material or a subsequent interpolation, either by the original author or by a later redactor.[4] This section includes the saying, 'Truly, truly, I say to you unless you eat the flesh of the Son of Man and drink his blood, you do not have life in you . . .' (John 6.53). Many who would excise these verses would do so on the ground that the earlier sayings are sapiential in nature, while the later verses have a more decidedly sacramental character. But there is another reason why at least part of this later material may be an addition to the original core. While the concept of eating flesh might have been difficult for a Jew to comprehend, the concept of drinking blood would have been an abomination. Thus it seems more likely that this part of the discourse would have been appended later, in a Gentile environment, and would not have formed part of the earlier Jewish stratum.

It seems possible, therefore, that the writer of the Fourth Gospel knew of a primitive tradition in which Jesus associated bread with his flesh, and this in the context of a feeding miracle rather than the Last Supper. But did any other early Christians know of such a tradition, or is it a peculiarity of this Gospel? Let us take a look.

The *Didache*

The *Didache* or 'Teaching of the Twelve Apostles' is commonly thought to be a very early Christian text, perhaps as old as the canonical Gospels

---

[2] The earliest to suggest this seems to have been J. H. Bernard, *A Critical and Exegetical Commentary on the Gospel according to John*, International Critical Commentary 29 (T & T Clark, Edinburgh 1928), pp. [clxx–clxxi]; see also Raymond E. Brown, *The Gospel According to John, i–xii*, Anchor Bible Commentary (Doubleday, Garden City, NY 1966), p. 285: 'it is possible that we have preserved in vi 51 the Johannine form of the words of institution'.

[3] See, for example, Brown, *The Gospel According to John, i–xii*, p. 285.

[4] For a summary of the debate, see Francis J. Moloney, *The Johannine Son of Man* (2nd edn, Libreria Ateneo Salesiano, Rome 1978), pp. 93ff.

themselves. Chapters 9 and 10 contain what appear to be prayers for use at a eucharistic meal, accompanied by brief directions.[5] This meal includes a cup (apparently of wine rather than water,[6] as the accompanying prayer refers to 'the holy vine of David') as well as bread. The bread and wine are not described here as being either the body and blood of Christ or the flesh and blood of Christ but simply as spiritual food and drink, and so offer us little help in this regard. It is to be noted, however, that this material does not associate the meal with the Last Supper or with Jesus' death in any way. Instead, the prayers speak of Jesus as bringing life, knowledge, and eternal life – themes that are also characteristic of the Fourth Gospel.[7] And to this we may add that Chapter 9 also uses the word 'fragment' when speaking of the bread rather than the normal Greek word for a loaf – and fragments are explicitly mentioned in the various feeding stories in the Gospels but not in the Last Supper narratives. Could it be that behind the text in the *Didache* is a remembrance of spiritual food and drink being associated with one of those stories? That suggestion may not be very convincing on its own, but let us go on to other early Christian writers.

Ignatius of Antioch

When Ignatius of Antioch mentions the eucharist, writing in the early second century, it is Christ's flesh that he speaks of and not his body. He says, 'Take care, therefore, to have one eucharist, for there is one flesh of our Lord Jesus Christ and one cup for union in his blood' (*Philadelphians* 4). Notice that, while he includes a cup along with the reference to flesh, he does not describe the contents (which may have been wine or water – he is not explicit about this) directly as blood. In another letter he also criticizes some because 'they abstain from eucharist and prayer, because they do not confess the eucharist to be flesh of our Saviour Jesus Christ, which suffered for our sins, which the Father by his goodness raised up' (*Smyrnaeans* 7.1). His choice of the word 'flesh' rather than 'body' suggests an affinity with the eucharistic tradition behind the

---

[5] For the Greek text and an English translation, see Kurt Niederwimmer, *The Didache: A Commentary* (Fortress Press, Minneapolis 1998), pp. 139–67. For the debate about the nature of the meal described in these particular chapters, see Bradshaw, *Eucharistic Origins*, ch. 2; and also below, pp. 39–44.

[6] On early eucharistic practices where water was used rather than wine, see Bradshaw, *Eucharistic Origins*, pp. 51–5.

[7] See Johannes Betz, 'The Eucharist in the Didache', in Jonathan A. Draper (ed.), *The Didache in Modern Research* (Brill, Leiden/New York 1996), pp. 244–75.

Fourth Gospel rather than that of the Synoptics or Paul, which he shows no sign of knowing.

Justin Martyr

Similar language is also used by Justin Martyr in the middle of the second century: 'not as common bread or common drink do we receive these things; but just as our Saviour Jesus Christ, being incarnate through [the] word of God, took both flesh and blood for our salvation, so too we have been taught that the food over which thanks have been given through [a] word of prayer which is from him, from which our blood and flesh are fed by transformation, is both the flesh and blood of that incarnate Jesus' (*First Apology* 66.2). Here Justin is more explicit in his association of the contents of the cup with the blood of Jesus than was Ignatius, but shares the same tradition, reflected in the Fourth Gospel, that remembered Jesus speaking about his flesh rather than body.

Justin, however, is the first writer outside the New Testament to reveal knowledge of another tradition that did speak about body and blood. For, in addition to the words I have just cited, he goes on to say: 'the apostles in the memoirs composed by them, which are called Gospels, have handed down what was commanded them: that Jesus having taken bread, having given thanks, said, "Do this in my remembrance; this is my body"; and similarly having taken the cup and having given thanks, said, "This is my blood"; and gave to them alone' (*First Apology* 66.3). Justin here claims to be quoting from 'the Gospels', by which it might seem that he was familiar with the Synoptic texts themselves. But none of them record as the words of Jesus, 'Do this in my remembrance; this is my body' – at least not in that order; and the only one of them to contain the words 'Do this in my remembrance' at all is the Gospel of Luke, and then only in the manuscripts that contain the longer version of the Last Supper narrative, and they do not record Jesus' words over the cup as 'This is my blood', but as 'This cup is the new covenant in my blood . . .' Yet in the one place in his writings where it is certain that Justin is quoting Luke's Gospel, it is the so-called Western Text that he knows, the manuscript tradition that contains the shorter version of the institution narrative lacking the command to 'do this in my remembrance'.[8] So it is almost certainly not from the Gospels as known to us that Justin has actually drawn this saying, but from some other source, most likely a collection of

---

[8] See Helmut Koester, *Ancient Christian Gospels: Their History and Development* (SCM Press, London 1990), pp. 360–402, esp. p. 365.

sayings of Jesus that had these words in a somewhat different form. This would help explain why so many of the other features of the Synoptic Last Supper narrative fail to make an appearance in Justin's writings. There is, for example, no mention of the words having been said on the night before he died, or of any of the interpretative phrases that form part of the sayings in the New Testament versions, such as 'body *given for you*' or 'blood *poured out for you*'.

Perhaps even more significant than these omissions is that there is no reference to the action of the breaking of the bread, which is recorded in all of the Synoptic texts and in Paul's account of the Last Supper in 1 Corinthians 11. Not only is this missing from Justin's recollection of Jesus here but it is also not explicitly mentioned in Justin's two accounts of actual Christian eucharistic practice in this same section of his work, although it can be said to be implied there (*First Apology* 65, 67). Now the one place in the New Testament where breaking is not mentioned in relation to Jesus giving thanks over bread is in the account of the miraculous feeding of the multitude with loaves and fishes in John 6. Could it be that the tradition which Justin knows links Jesus' saying with a version of that story rather than the Last Supper? There is also another similarity between that story and Justin's vocabulary. When Justin recalls that Jesus 'similarly' took the cup, the Greek word that he uses is not *homoios*, found in the Last Supper accounts of Luke and Paul, but *hosautos*, used in John 6.11 of Jesus 'similarly' taking the fish.[9] Admittedly, this variation could be just a coincidence, but the omission of a reference to breaking the bread looks more significant, especially when we add to it the fact that Irenaeus, writing later in the second century, appears to have been familiar with a similar tradition.

Irenaeus

Like Justin, Irenaeus makes no mention of the context of the eucharistic sayings when he quotes them, neither of the Last Supper nor of the impending passion. He simply says: 'He took that created thing, bread, and gave thanks, saying, "This is my body." And the cup likewise, which is part of that creation to which we belong, he declared his blood . . .' (*Adversus haereses* 4.17.5). Not only, like Justin, does his version of the sayings lack any of the interpretative phrases attached to them in the New Testament accounts, but there is again no mention of the breaking of the bread. True,

---

[9] Justin also uses this same link word in reference to the bread and cup of the eucharist in his *Dialogue with Trypho* 41.3.

Irenaeus shows no knowledge of the use of 'flesh' rather than 'body', but the close parallels between his account of Jesus' words and Justin's suggest that both are drawing on a catechetical tradition as to the origin of the eucharist that has come down independently of the Gospel texts themselves and that did not link it with the narrative of the Last Supper.

Unlike Justin, however, Irenaeus is definitely also familiar with at least one of the Gospel accounts of the Last Supper themselves, as he quotes part of the Matthean version elsewhere in the same work.[10] Nevertheless, it is upon its eschatological statement about drinking in the kingdom that he comments, passing over in silence the reference to the 'blood of the new covenant, which will be poured out for many for forgiveness of sins' and not making any explicit connection to the eucharist. Indeed, although at one point in his writing Irenaeus does move from mention of redemption with the blood of the Lord to the cup of the eucharist as being communion in his blood,[11] he does not develop the link further. Like Justin, he sees the eucharistic body and blood of Jesus primarily in terms of nourishment for human flesh, and so giving it the hope of resurrection to eternal life, rather than as that which was sacrificed for human salvation. Thus he says: 'as the bread, which is produced from the earth, when it receives the invocation of God, is no longer common bread but the eucharist, consisting of two realities, earthly and heavenly; so also our bodies, when they receive the eucharist, are no longer corruptible, having the hope of the resurrection to eternity' (*Adversus haereses* 4.18.5). And later he goes on to speak of our flesh being 'nourished from the body and blood of the Lord' and 'nourished by the cup which is his blood, and receives increase from the bread which is his body' (5.2.3).

North Africa: Tertullian and Cyprian

It is therefore not until we get to Tertullian in North Africa at the end of the second century that we find a Christian writer outside the New

---

[10] 'When he had given thanks over the cup, and had drunk of it, and given it to the disciples, he said to them: "Drink of it, all [of you]: this is my blood of the new covenant, which will be poured out for many for forgiveness of sins. But I tell you, I will not drink henceforth of the fruit of this vine until that day when I will drink it new with you in my Father's kingdom"' (*Adversus haereses* 5.33.1). We may note the use of the future tense here 'which will be poured out', a reading which recurs in a number of other renderings of the Matthean narrative, but also the description of Jesus drinking before giving the cup to the disciples or saying the words, something not otherwise found in Matthew.

[11] 'Now if this flesh is not saved, neither did the Lord redeem us with his blood, nor is the cup of the eucharist communion in his blood, nor is the bread which we break communion in his body' (*Adversus haereses* 5.2.2).

Testament who locates Jesus' words in their paschal context and refers to the covenant, even if Tertullian does not mention either giving thanks or breaking the bread. He says: 'Having taken bread and given it to the disciples, he made it his body by saying, "This is my body" . . . Similarly, when mentioning the cup and making the covenant to be sealed by his blood, he affirms the reality of his body' (*Adversus Marcionem* 4.40.3).

His fellow countryman Cyprian in the middle of the third century goes further and quotes two of the New Testament accounts of the Last Supper in one of his letters. He first cites part of the Matthean version: 'For, on the eve of his passion, taking the cup, he blessed, and gave (it) to his disciples, saying, "Drink of this, all [of you]; for this is the blood of the covenant, which will be poured out for many for forgiveness of sins. I tell you, I shall not drink again of this fruit of the vine until that day when I shall drink new wine with you in my Father's kingdom." '[12] A little later in the same letter, Cyprian quotes Paul's account of the Last Supper in 1 Corinthians 11. 'The Lord Jesus, on the night he was betrayed, took bread, and gave thanks, and broke it, and said, "This is my body, which shall be given for you: do this in my remembrance." In the same way also after supper, he took the cup, saying, "This cup is the new covenant in my blood: do this, as often as you drink it, in my remembrance." For as often as you eat this bread and drink the cup, you proclaim the Lord's death until he comes.'[13]

Not only does Cyprian quote these texts in full, but the whole basis of the argument in the letter in which they are cited is that Christians are obliged to imitate Jesus when they celebrate the eucharist, and do exactly what he did at the Last Supper. This includes using wine and water mixed together and not just water alone, as some of his contemporaries were doing. Naturally this argument runs into some difficulties when it comes to the hour of celebration, for Cyprian's church clearly has the eucharist in the morning and not the evening, but he does his best: 'It was fitting for Christ to offer about the evening of the day, so that the very hour of sacrifice might show the setting and evening of the world, as it is written in Exodus, "And all the people of the synagogue of the children of Israel shall kill it in the evening"; and again in the Psalms, "the lifting up of my hands

---

[12] *Epistula* 63.9. There are two interesting variants here from the text of the Gospel as it is generally known to us. He uses the verb 'bless' over the cup instead of 'give thanks', a variant that also turns up in the Roman Canon of the Mass, and also the future tense 'which will be poured out for you', instead of the present tense. This second variant also occurs in Irenaeus' citation of this passage and in what is known as the Old Latin translation of the Gospel.

[13] *Epistula* 63.10. Here Cyprian has another variant, using the future in connection with the bread, 'which will be given up (*tradetur*) for you', against the usual text which has simply 'which is for you'.

[as] an evening sacrifice". But we celebrate the resurrection of the Lord in the morning' (*Epistula* 63.16).

There appear to be two main reasons why Cyprian drew on the New Testament texts in this way when his predecessors had not. First, those texts were now coming to be regarded not merely as apostolic writings but as authoritative Scripture, which therefore tended to override whatever might be contained in other written or oral traditions. Second, Cyprian's church faced a period of persecution, when some of its members might be required to offer the sacrifice of their lives. In this pastoral context, therefore, it was more important than ever to link the celebration of the eucharistic rite with Jesus' own sacrificial oblation of his body and blood: 'For if Jesus Christ, our Lord and God, is himself the high priest of God the Father and first offered himself as a sacrifice to the Father, and commanded this to be done in his remembrance, then that priest truly functions in the place of Christ who imitates what Christ did and then offers a true and full sacrifice in the church to God the Father, if he thus proceeds to offer according to what he sees Christ himself to have offered.'[14]

Continuing independent traditions?

On the basis of this admittedly limited evidence, it would appear that it was not until the third century that the New Testament texts came to dominate what was thought and said by Christians about the institution of the eucharist. Yet even after that, liturgical formulae did not always conform their wording of the narrative of the Last Supper precisely to what was recorded in those venerable documents, but variants continue to flourish.

Thus, the institution narrative in the eucharistic prayer of the so-called *Apostolic Tradition* of Hippolytus[15] begins by paralleling the form in Justin Martyr ('taking bread, giving thanks to you, he said'), with its omission of the conjunction 'and' and with its lack of any explicit reference to the supper or to breaking the bread. But then, when it cites the words of Jesus himself, it has 'Take, eat, this is my body that will be broken for you' – a mixture of those found in Matthew ('Take, eat, this is my body') and those in some manuscripts of 1 Corinthians ('This is my body that is broken for you'), but without the latter's command to repeat the action. The use

---

[14] *Epistula* 63.14. See further Bradshaw, *Eucharistic Origins*, pp. 110–12.
[15] See Paul F. Bradshaw, Maxwell E. Johnson and L. Edward Phillips, *The Apostolic Tradition: A Commentary* (Fortress Press, Minneapolis 2002), pp. 37–48, and on the critical questions surrounding this church order also below, pp. 45–6.

of the future tense, 'will be broken', is unusual in early Christian citations of the words of Jesus, although we have noted that 'will be given up for you' is found in Cyprian's quotation of 1 Corinthians 11.24, and 'will be broken' also appears again in the institution narrative of the eucharistic prayer quoted by Ambrose of Milan in the fourth century (*De sacramentis* 4.21). The words over the cup ('This is my blood that is shed for you. When you do this, you do my remembrance') offer no precise parallel with any one of the canonical accounts, although 'that is shed for you' corresponds to what is found in the longer text of Luke, and the final command echoes 1 Corinthians 11.25. It should also be noted that the account lacks any statement that Jesus then distributed the bread and wine to his disciples.

On the other hand, the eucharistic prayer in the mid-fourth-century *Sacramentary of Sarapion*[16] does mention the night when Jesus was betrayed, the supper, and also the breaking of the bread, although strangely omits any reference to Jesus 'blessing' or 'giving thanks'. The narrative appears to be chiefly a combination of components from 1 Corinthians 11 and Matthew's version, with words and phrases from the bread unit copied into the cup unit, and vice versa, so as to increase the parallelism of the two. However, as one construction that does not appear verbatim in any of the New Testament versions also turns up in some other earlier Christian writings, this suggests that at least part of it may again be drawn from an older independent tradition rather than having simply been manufactured out of the New Testament material. The words over the cup, 'Take drink . . .', a form that is found in none of the New Testament versions, might be thought to be simply an attempt to parallel the Matthean version of the words over the bread, 'Take, eat, this is my body'. But because the same words are also found in the anonymous treatise *In Sanctum Pascha*, previously regarded as the work of Hippolytus but now thought to date from the second century,[17] in writings of Origen in the third century before he went to Caesarea (*Commentarius in Evangelium Ioannis* 32.24; *Homiliae in Jeremiam* 12), in Eusebius of Caesarea in the fourth century (*Demonstratio evangelica* 8.1.28), and the *Mystagogical Catecheses* attributed to Cyril of Jerusalem (4.1), sources that are both geographically and temporally so disparate, this may well be yet another form of an independent sayings tradition.

---

[16] See Maxwell E. Johnson, *The Prayers of Sarapion of Thmuis: A Literary, Liturgical, and Theological Analysis*, Orientalia Christiana Analecta 249 (Pontifico Istituto Orientale, Rome 1995), pp. 219–33.

[17] Text in Pierre Nautin (ed.), *Homélies pascales I*, Sources chrétiennes 27 (Éditions du Cerf, Paris 1950), no. 49.

Everything that we have examined so far would seem to point towards the conclusion that it was not the New Testament accounts of the Last Supper that originally shaped what Christians thought and said about Jesus' words concerning his flesh and blood or body and blood, nor even an oral tradition that paralleled those written accounts, but a quite independent tradition or traditions. This strand did not at first link Jesus' sayings specifically with the night before he died or the Last Supper, nor did it include the sort of interpretative phrases that we find in the New Testament versions, such as 'body *given for you*' or 'blood *poured out for you*', that relate them to his sacrificial death. And even when the New Testament did begin to be regarded as authoritative Scripture, it did not manage completely to efface some elements in these earlier independent catechetical versions from liturgical usage, but they continue to find a place in a number of eucharistic prayers.

This claim, however, may still sound improbable. Granted that other traditions may have existed prior to the books that came to make up the New Testament being written, nevertheless those books were widely known to Christians long before the third century. Not every one of them may have been current in every region of the ancient Christian world, but one or other of the written accounts of the Last Supper would surely have been known and would have affected how the story was told, would it not? An independent tradition of eucharistic sayings could surely not have survived and ignored the association of the words over bread and cup with Christ's sacrificial death that is made both in the Synoptic Gospels and in 1 Corinthians as soon as these writings began to be disseminated.

That may seem a likely scenario, but is not perhaps exactly how things were in early Christianity. For instance, Paul's letter to the Romans was obviously widely circulated and well known to Christians in many places, and so one might expect that the baptismal theology of chapter 6, of dying and rising with Christ, would have played a significant part in shaping the language and thought about the meaning of baptism in the early centuries. But that is not the case, and a baptismal theology of new birth, generally related to what we find in John 3, appears to have dominated the scene instead, as much in the West as in the East.[18] In the light of this, it perhaps appears less remarkable that much Christian thinking

---

[18] See Maxwell E. Johnson, 'Baptism as "New Birth *Ex Aqua et Spiritu*": A Preliminary Investigation of Western Liturgical Sources', in Robert F. Taft and Gabriele Winkler (eds), *Comparative Liturgy Fifty Years after Anton Baumstark*, Orientalia Christiana Analecta 265 (Pontifico Istituto Orientale, Rome 2001), pp. 787–807, reprinted in Johnson, *Worship: Rites, Feasts, and Reflections* (Pastoral Press, Portland, OR 2004), pp. 37–62; Dominic Serra, 'Baptism: Birth in the Spirit or Dying with Christ', *Ecclesia Orans* 22 (2005), pp. 295–314.

about eucharistic presence in the first and second centuries also continued to follow what might be described as Johannine rather than Synoptic or Pauline paths. In this regard we may also note that pictorial representations of the eucharist found in the Roman catacombs allude to the feeding miracles of Jesus and not to the Last Supper.[19]

The New Testament accounts

In any case, the Last Supper version of the eucharistic sayings of Jesus may not have been as widespread or dominant even in first-century Christianity as the existence of four accounts of it in the New Testament books may lead us to suppose. Obviously the tradition that Jesus spoke these words on the night that he was betrayed was known to Paul when he wrote his first letter to the Corinthian Christians some twenty years after the death of Jesus, as he quotes them in the letter, with the interpretative phrases that relate them to that death and with the command to repeat the action in remembrance of Jesus (11.23–6). He does not, however, state specifically that the supper was a Passover meal. The narrative, he claims, he 'received from the Lord'. New Testament scholars debate just what Paul means on the occasions when he says that certain traditions come from the Lord.[20] He cannot mean directly from the earthly Jesus, as he never knew him. The only possibilities, therefore, seem to be either from a Christian source that he believes to have preserved a trustworthy version of what Jesus actually said and did, or alternatively by some sort of direct revelation. But in either case we have no reason to jump to the conclusion that it was a universal or well-known tradition within early Christianity. Indeed, his Corinthian correspondents do not seem to be very familiar with it and need reminding, even though Paul says he had already told them it previously.

But what about the Synoptic Gospel accounts? Does not the fact that Jesus' words are recorded in all three Gospels as having been uttered at the Last Supper show that this tradition was widespread in the first century? Let us take a closer look. New Testament scholars have long recognized that there is what has been called a 'double strand' within these Last Supper narratives: on the one hand, an eschatological focus, represented

---

[19] See the examples described in Geoffrey Wainwright, *Eucharist and Eschatology* (Epworth Press, London 1971), pp. 42–3.

[20] Cf. Galatians 1.12; 1 Corinthians 7.10; and for a discussion of the question, see, for example, C. K. Barrett, *A Commentary on the First Epistle to the Corinthians* (A & C Black, London 1968), pp. 264–6.

chiefly by the statement, 'I shall not drink of the fruit of the vine . . .', in the three Gospel texts, and on the other hand, the words over the bread and cup relating them to Jesus' body and blood. While these scholars might disagree as to whether or not these words go back to the historical Last Supper, they generally share a consensus that they would already have been combined with the eschatological theme in the eucharistic practice of the Palestinian Christian communities prior to Pauline influence.[21] However, over twenty years ago the French scholar Xavier Léon-Dufour, in a book to which too little attention has been paid, proposed that the two strands were transmitted through two distinct literary genres and he implied that their combination was actually the work of the evangelists themselves, although he did not develop the consequences of this latter thesis.[22] He was not the first to suggest that the eucharistic sayings of Jesus had been interpolated into an earlier narrative of Jesus' last Passover meal with his disciples,[23] but was the first to offer a plausible explanation for this phenomenon.

If we examine the Synoptic texts themselves, we can easily see some signs of the division to which Léon-Dufour and others have pointed. In Mark's account, in chapter 14, there is the repetition of the phrase 'as they were eating' in verses 18 and 22, which might be thought to suggest a combination of two separate beginnings of a narrative. Equally odd in this text is the fact that the disciples are said to have drunk from the cup before Jesus says the words that interpret its meaning (14.23–4). And if we turn to Luke's narrative, we find another oddity, at least if we accept the longer version of the text as authentic: not only are two cups mentioned, one before and one after supper (22.17, 20), but also there is the apparently contradictory situation of Jesus declaring in verse 18 that he will no longer drink of the fruit of the vine and then in verse 20 of his doing so.

So, then, let us follow the lead suggested by Léon-Dufour and attempt to untangle the two strands. If we separate the eucharistic sayings and the material in which they are embedded from the rest of the Last Supper narratives, what we have left are accounts of a Passover meal containing eschatological statements by Jesus that are complete in themselves, with

---

[21] See for example R. H. Fuller, 'The Double Origin of the Eucharist', *Biblical Research* 8 (1963), pp. 60–72; A. J. B. Higgins, *The Lord's Supper in the New Testament* (SCM Press, London 1952), pp. 56–63; Eduard Schweizer, *The Lord's Supper according to the New Testament* (Fortress Press, Philadelphia 1967), p. 25.

[22] Xavier Léon-Dufour, *Le Partage du pain eucharistique selon le Nouveau Testament* (Éditions du Seuil, Paris 1982); ET: *Sharing the Eucharistic Bread* (Paulist Press, New York 1987), pp. 82ff.

[23] See, for example, Rudolf Bultmann, *The History of the Synoptic Tradition* (Blackwell, Oxford 1963), p. 265; S. Dockx, 'Le récit du repas pascal. Marc 14,17–26', *Biblica* 46 (1965), pp. 445–53.

no signs of dislocation, as follows (the eucharistic sayings strand being indicated by the use of italics and the longer version of Luke by square brackets):

MARK 14   LUKE 22

¹⁷And when it was evening, he came with the twelve. ¹⁸And as they were at table eating, Jesus said, 'Truly, I say to you that one of you will betray me, one eating with me.' ¹⁹They began to be sorrowful and to say to him one by one, 'Is it I?' ²⁰He said to them, '(It is) one of the twelve, one dipping with me in the dish. ²¹For the Son of man goes as it is written concerning him, but woe to that man by whom the Son of man is betrayed. (It would have been) good for him if that man had not been born.' *²²And as they were eating, having taken bread, having blessed, he broke (it) and gave (it) to them and said, 'Take; this is my body.'* ²³And having taken a cup, having given thanks, he gave (it) to them, and they all drank from it. ²⁴And he said to them, *'This is my blood of the [new] covenant, which (is) poured out for many.* ²⁵Truly, I say to you, I shall not drink again of the fruit of the vine until that day when I drink it new in the kingdom of God.'

¹⁴And when the hour came, he sat at table, and the apostles with him. ¹⁵And he said to them, 'With desire I have desired to eat this Passover with you before I suffer, ¹⁶for I say to you, I shall not/never again eat it until it is fulfilled in the kingdom of God.' ¹⁷And having accepted a cup, having given thanks, he said, 'Take this, and share it among you; ¹⁸for I say to you, I shall not drink from now on from the fruit of the vine until the kingdom of God comes.' *¹⁹And having taken bread, having given thanks, he broke (it) and gave (it) to them, saying, 'This is my body [which (is) given for you. Do this in my remembrance.' ²⁰And the cup likewise after the supper, saying, 'This cup (is) the new covenant in my blood, which (is) poured out for you].* ²¹But behold the hand of the one betraying me (is) with me on the table. For the Son of man goes according to what has been determined, but woe to that man by whom he is betrayed.' ²²And they began to question one another, which of them . . .

Mark and Luke may have variations in the order in which the various sayings are arranged, but they are telling basically the same story. Mark has the conversation about betrayal first, while Luke begins with a statement by Jesus about not eating of the Passover again. Both then follow with Jesus taking a cup and saying he will also not drink of the cup again, and Luke has the conversation about betrayal afterwards. Thus the focus of these Supper narratives is on eschatology and upon impending betrayal. They make total sense without the body and blood sayings, and those sayings therefore look like secondary insertions.

In the case of Mark's version, what seems to have happened is that the Evangelist has worked the eucharistic sayings material into this pre-existent narrative where he could best fit it. He thus inserted the bread saying unit immediately after the discussion on betrayal, and the blood saying after the existing reference to the cup. This has resulted, as I said earlier, in the repetition of a beginning, 'as they were eating', and of the cup being shared before the interpretative words are spoken. Matthew has tried to solve this difficulty in his version by applying an editorial hand to Mark's text and converting the narrative statement, 'they all drank of it', into the command, 'Drink of it, all' (26.27–8).

Luke appears to have done something slightly different from Mark in combining the two sets of material. But here, things get somewhat complicated because of the existence of two quite different manuscript traditions of Luke's narrative, a shorter and a longer one.[24] Since either of these might be the original one, we need to be able to account for the combination in both cases. If we assume first that the longer one is the original, then Luke appears to have acquired a separate version of the sayings narrative from Mark, as there are several differences between the two: Luke has 'given thanks' where Mark has 'blessed'; Luke does not have 'Take' but does add 'which is given for you. Do this in my remembrance' to the saying, 'This is my body'; and while Mark has, 'This is my blood of the new covenant which is poured out for many', as the words over the cup, Luke has the variant, 'This cup is the new covenant in my blood which is poured out for you.' Luke also treats the material differently, and appears simply to have dropped the sayings narrative into the eschatological Last Supper as a single block, and it is this that has produced the two cups and the apparently contradictory situation of Jesus declaring in verse 18 that he will no longer drink of the fruit of the vine and then in verse 20 of his doing so.

On the other hand, the shorter version of Luke's text may be the original, with the longer being an expansion by a later hand. This has a shorter saying over the bread, and lacks entirely the eucharistic saying over the cup. Although in the course of the twentieth century the weight of scholarly opinion has swung in favour of regarding the longer form as authentic, chiefly because of the strong manuscript support for it, it seems to me more likely that the shorter is what the Evangelist wrote,

---

[24] For details, see Joachim Jeremias, *The Eucharistic Words of Jesus* (SCM Press, London 1966), pp. 139–52.

because otherwise there appears to be no good reason for the shorter ever to have existed at all. Who would have wanted to curtail the longer account? Moreover, while it was once commonly thought that it would have been anomalous for anyone to have composed a Last Supper account that placed cup first and bread second, because that would have contradicted the order followed in early Christian liturgical practice, there is now a growing body of opinion which believes that just such an order was not unknown among the earliest Christian practices.[25] If this were so, then it is easy to see how the Evangelist, with his eschatological narrative already containing a mention of the paschal meal and its cup with a saying over it, might have read Mark's version and thought that he ought also to include the saying over the bread in his account, and so simply slipped in the saying copied from Mark, changing the verb 'bless' to the more familiar 'give thanks' as he did so.[26]

Incidentally, this explanation also provides a solution to two perceived problems with the received text. First, some scholars have claimed that the Last Supper cannot have been a Passover meal because unleavened bread (*azuma*) would have been used on that occasion and not ordinary bread (*artos*). Against this, Joachim Jeremias argued strongly that the latter word could also be used for unleavened bread.[27] However, if the sayings were in truth a later interpolation into the narrative, no doubts can be cast on the Last Supper having been a Passover meal on the grounds of the choice of word. Second, there is the unusual 'mixed' usage of 'bless' over the bread but 'give thanks' over the cup that we find in Mark and Matthew. In spite of a persisting misconception among many New Testament scholars that these verbs are merely synonyms that might be employed interchangeably, they actually refer to two quite different Jewish liturgical constructions.[28] One might well have expected that a tradition that employed 'bless' over the bread would have done the same over the cup, just as the Lukan and Pauline versions use 'thank' for both. However, if Mark were grafting his sayings material on to a source where 'thank' was already in use for the eschatological saying over the cup, it would account

---

[25] See Bradshaw, *Eucharistic Origins*, ch. 3.

[26] The suggestion that Luke simply added Mark's saying over the bread to his Passover material has already been made by others: see Henry Chadwick, 'The Shorter Text of Luke xxii 15–20', *Harvard Theological Review* 50 (1957), pp. 249–58; B. P. Robinson, 'The Place of the Emmaus Story in Luke-Acts', *New Testament Studies* 30 (1984), pp. 481–97, esp. pp. 488–90.

[27] Jeremias, *The Eucharistic Words of Jesus*, pp. 62–6.

[28] See further Paul F. Bradshaw, *Daily Prayer in the Early Church* (SPCK, London 1981/Oxford University Press, New York 1982, reprinted Wipf & Stock, Eugene, OR 2008), pp. 11–16; idem, *The Search for the Origins of Christian Worship*, pp. 43–4.

for his retaining that verb in relation to the new cup saying that he added, while at the same time inserting the full unit concerning the bread from a source that had used the verb 'bless' for both.

In other words, according to this scenario, we do not really have four independent witnesses in the New Testament to the Last Supper tradition as containing the sayings of Jesus about body and blood. We have one witness, Paul, to a tradition that Mark also hears about, though it is not in his core narrative of the passion, and so he adds it rather clumsily, and it is then copied, to varying degrees, by Matthew and Luke. This suggests that, far from the two strands of the tradition having been integrated at a very early stage, there were Christian communities in the second half of the first century that still did not connect the tradition of the sayings of Jesus about his body and blood over bread and cup directly with a Passover meal at which he made an eschatological statement, nor even with the night before he died.

The emergence of the eucharist

How, then, do I think that the eucharistic sayings of Jesus developed and the early Christian eucharistic practices emerged? I believe that the regular sharing of food was fundamental to the common life of the first Christian communities, as it apparently had been to Jesus' own mission. At these meals they would have experienced an eschatological anticipation of God's kingdom, one of the primary marks of which was that the hungry are fed and many come from East and West to feast (Matthew 8.11; Luke 13.29), and they would have responded by calling upon Jesus to return, crying *Marana tha* (1 Corinthians 16.22; *Didache* 10.6; Revelation 22.20). They would have recalled stories of Jesus eating – not just with his disciples, but scandalously with tax-collectors and sinners. They would have recollected that he had miraculously fed large multitudes with small quantities of food. And they would have remembered that he had at least once, perhaps in relation to one of these feeding miracles, associated bread with his own flesh. At least some communities of impoverished Christians, whose staple food would have been bread and little else and whose meals generally did not include wine, came to associate what they called the breaking of bread[29] with feeding on the flesh of Jesus. In other cases, where wealthy members of the local congregation would entertain their brothers and sisters in the faith to a more substantial supper in their homes each week, either on the eve of the Sabbath or at its

---

[29] For a discussion of this term, see Bradshaw, *Eucharistic Origins*, pp. 55–9.

conclusion, the bread and wine of the meal might have been thought of as simply 'spiritual food and drink' (as in the *Didache*), or as the flesh and blood of Jesus, although in some Greek-speaking circles the expression 'body and blood' came to be preferred. In neither case, because they did not associate what they were doing specifically with the Last Supper or with the annual Passover meal, did they apparently experience any qualms about doing it much more often than once a year or feel the necessity to adhere strictly to the order of that meal in their own practices.

Someone, however, possibly even St Paul himself, did begin to associate the sayings of Jesus with the supper that took place on the night before he died, and interpreted them as referring to the sacrifice of his body and blood and to the new covenant that would be made through his death. This interpretation had some influence within the churches founded by Paul and possibly beyond. It certainly reached the author of Mark's Gospel, who inserted a version of the sayings into his already existing supper narrative, perhaps because he was compiling his account of Jesus in Rome, where the Christians were particularly subject to sporadic persecution and so the association of their own spiritual meals with the sacrificed body and blood of their Saviour would have been especially encouraging to believers facing possible martyrdom themselves, however novel to them was this juxtaposition of the two traditions. But this combination does not otherwise seem to have been widely known in early Christianity. It was only much later, as the New Testament books gained currency and authority, that it began to shape both the catechesis and the liturgy of the churches, and to shift the focus of eucharistic thought from feeding to sacrifice.

Does any of this matter? Is it important whether the ultimate roots of Jesus' sayings may lie in the life-giving feeding of those who were hungry rather than in primary association with his imminent death? Did not that sacrificial death also come to be viewed by Christians as life-giving, and therefore to an equal degree as spiritually nourishing? Was anything really lost? I think so. While I believe it was, and is, perfectly legitimate for Christians to interpret Jesus' sayings in relation to his death, whenever and wherever they may have first been uttered, yet I believe a valuable balanced insight was lost by an excessive focus on the power of his sacrificed body and blood and a consequent diminishing of the value of his living and nourishing flesh and blood. In particular, it led in the course of time to a decline in the reception of communion, as that came to be seen as less important for believers than the offering of the eucharistic sacrifice – to a disproportionate emphasis, if you like, on altar rather than on table.

2

Receiving communion

The roots of communion at home: feeding the hungry?

Justin Martyr in the middle of the second century is the first Christian writer to describe the practice of sending bread – and in this case at least apparently wine also – by the hands of the deacons from the Sunday eucharistic celebration to those unable to be present at it (*First Apology* 65.5; 67.5), while Tertullian at the end of that century refers to bread being carried home for consumption during the week by those who had been present at the celebration (*Ad uxorem* 2.5; cf. also *De oratione* 19). Both these practices continue to be attested by later sources, with occasional references to wine being included in what was carried home by communicants.[1] What was it, however, that gave rise to these customs? It has been suggested that the second – the taking home of consecrated elements for consumption during the week – came into being independently of the first around the beginning of the third century as a response to a desire for more frequent communion during times of persecution.[2] But Tertullian's reference to it seems to imply that it was already an established practice at that time, and sustained and widespread persecution did not occur until the middle of the century. Is it possible therefore that both belong together and are much older, arising in the first century out of the necessity for the poor in the Christian community to have their physical hunger satisfied every day, and being continued later with more token quantities of bread (and wine) as a way of continuing to feed spiritually on Christ each day?

When we attempt to visualize the Last Supper, many of us are unconsciously influenced by Renaissance artistic depictions into imagining the disciples as being seated at one long table, with Jesus in the centre,

---

[1] *Apostolic Tradition* 38A is unclear, but may refer to preserving wine at home: see Bradshaw, Johnson and Phillips, *The Apostolic Tradition: A Commentary*, pp. 184–5. See also below, p. 26, for a later instance.
[2] W. H. Freestone, *The Sacrament Reserved*, Alcuin Club Collections 21 (Mowbray, London/ Oxford 1917), pp. 33–4.

whereas not only that occasion but also the subsequent formal eucharistic meals of the early Christians would very probably have conformed to the cultural norms of their age, with the company reclining on couches arranged around three sides of the room and eating from small tables and the host placed at one end.[3] Indeed, the use of a single table and the practice of standing for the eucharist probably only arose when the serving of a full meal ceased. We may also reasonably presume that at these early ritual suppers Christians would have continued to adhere to the prevailing social conventions in other respects too, not least with regard to their treatment of the poor.

In the complex world of Greco-Roman culture in the time of Jesus, the wealthy might invite to dinner with them not only friends of equal standing, but also people of lower social status – their dependent clients, although often these would be seated apart and the food and drink served to them would be of a quite different quality from that being enjoyed by the host and his more privileged guests.[4] Similarly, there were times when clients would have to make do with a charitable handout of food from their patron to take home rather than with a place at table.[5] Thus, it was within this cultural context that the leading members of each Christian community in the first few generations would have invited their fellow-believers, both rich and poor, to share regular eucharistic meals in their homes. Many of these communities apparently saw themselves as brothers and sisters within one family, a phenomenon that was not unknown in some other associations within that culture.[6] Not only is familial language used of them in the New Testament, but they also exchanged kisses with one another, an action normally only performed within that culture between very close friends or family members.[7] Apparently so real did this new relationship feel to some that they refused

---

[3] See further Blake Leyerle, 'Meal Customs in the Greco-Roman World', in Paul F. Bradshaw and Lawrence A. Hoffman (eds), *Passover and Easter: Origin and History to Modern Times* (University of Notre Dame Press, Notre Dame, IN 1999), pp. 29–61, here at pp. 30–4.

[4] See Ludwig Friedländer, *Roman Life and Manners under the Early Empire* (Routledge, London 1913), I, pp. 199ff.

[5] For references to primary sources, see Charles A. Bobertz, 'The Role of Patron in the *Cena Dominica* of Hippolytus' Apostolic Tradition', *Journal of Theological Studies* 44 (1993), pp. 170–84, here at pp. 175–6; Matthias Klinghardt, *Gemeinschaftsmahl und Mahlgemeinschaft* (Francke Verlag, Tübingen 1996), pp. 143–9.

[6] See Philip A. Harland, *Associations, Synagogues, and Congregations* (Fortress Press, Minneapolis 2003), pp. 30–3.

[7] See L. Edward Phillips, *The Ritual Kiss in Early Christian Worship*, Alcuin/GROW Joint Liturgical Study 36 (Grove Books, Nottingham 1996).

to exchange kisses any longer with members of their natural family who were not believers.[8]

In such communities we may naturally expect that what otherwise would have been the conventional social stratification at meals between rich and poor, men and women, would have disappeared, and all would have been treated equally at the eucharistic suppers (cf. Galatians 3.28: 'There is neither Jew nor Greek, there is neither slave nor free, there is neither male nor female; for you are all one in Christ Jesus'). However, this does not appear to have been the case everywhere. The apostle Paul rebukes the Corinthian church for perpetuating social distinctions between rich and poor, with the rich arriving first at the meals, bringing their provisions with them and consuming them without waiting for or sharing their food and drink with the poor.[9] There is also later evidence of continuing segregation by gender in some Christian assemblies (*Didascalia Apostolorum* 2.57), but not in others: Tertullian notes that the practice of kissing the 'brothers' could pose a problem for women married to unbelievers (*Ad uxorem* 2.4).

Nevertheless, even if the poor were not treated as equals in every Christian community, the concern to be charitable to the needy seems to have been adopted as a high priority within the early Christian movement – so much so indeed that Acts 6 tells of the burden that 'serving tables' placed upon the Twelve in Jerusalem and the consequent need to have others take on that ministry. There are also references within the New Testament to collections being made for those in need (Acts 24.17; Romans 15.25–8; 1 Corinthians 16.1–2; 2 Corinthians 8.3–5; 9.1ff.); and a similar practice is recorded by Justin Martyr as accompanying the weekly eucharist:

> Those who have provide for all those in need . . . And those who have the means and so desire give what they wish, each according to his own choice; and what is collected is deposited with the president. And he provides for both orphans and widows, and those in need through sickness or through other cause, and those who are in prison, and strangers sojourning, and, in a word, he becomes a protector for all those who are in want.
>
> (*First Apology* 67.1, 6–7)

---

[8] See Michael Penn, 'Performing Family: Ritual Kissing and the Construction of Early Christian Kinship', *Journal of Early Christian Studies* 10 (2002), pp. 151–74, esp. pp. 166–9.

[9] 1 Corinthians 11.17–22. See Peter Lampe, 'Das korinthische Herrenmahl im Schnittpunkt hellenistischrömischer Mahlpraxis und paulinischer Theologia Crucis (1 Kor 11,17–34)', *Zeitschrift für die Neutestamentliche Wissenschaft* 82 (1990–1), pp. 183–213; also his English article, 'The Eucharist: Identifying with Christ on the Cross', *Interpretation* 48 (1994), pp. 36–49.

The so-called *Apostolic Tradition* also gives instructions both about suppers being given for the benefit of the poor and about donations of food being made to them to take home (chapters 28, 30), both of which, as we have seen, were common cultural practices, while *Didache* 13.4 directs that in the absence of prophets in a Christian community to be the recipients of the firstfruits that have been offered, they are to be donated to the poor.

Although the reception of communion was restricted to the baptized (Justin Martyr, *First Apology* 66.1), this does not mean that charitable feeding was limited only to those persons. It is important to note that while *Apostolic Tradition* 27.1 directs that catechumens are not to 'sit at the table of the Lord with believers', chapter 26.2 apparently does include them in some eating and drinking, but with 'exorcized bread' and their own cup because they are not yet pure (cf. 26.1). The presence of a prohibition against the unbaptized sharing in the eucharist in *Didache* 9.5 could also be thought to imply that they were there at that event. In such contexts, therefore, it would seem that catechumens only became excluded from presence at the eucharistic action and restricted to the liturgy of the word once a full meal was no longer part of eucharistic practice.

The earliest Christian eucharistic meal, therefore, did not merely express symbolically the love that the believers had for one another but was itself a practical expression of that love, as those who had means fed those in the community who were hungry, sending them home with leftovers to sustain them during the week and distributing portions to those unable to be present. It was no wonder then that one of the names used to designate that meal in some Christian communities was *agape* – the Greek word for 'love'.[10]

Daily communion in the fourth century

It is impossible to know how widespread the custom of communion at home was during the first few centuries, but in North Africa in the third century we see signs of its reception at church becoming more frequent than appears originally to have been the case. All our early evidence points to 'the Lord's day' as being the normal weekly occasion for the eucharistic celebration, even if that were at first Saturday evening rather than Sunday morning. But Tertullian speaks of the distribution of communion, even if not a full eucharistic celebration, as being also a regular feature

---

[10] See Andrew B. McGowan, 'Naming the Feast: *Agape* and the Diversity of Early Christian Meals', *Studia Patristica* 30 (1997), pp. 314–18.

of the two station days, Wednesdays and Fridays,[11] and some years later Cyprian's language implies that, at least during a period of persecution, the eucharist might been celebrated more often still, even daily (*Epistulae* 5; 57.3).

Within fourth-century sources can be found plentiful references to at least some Christians receiving communion more often than once a week. However, when early Christian writers speak of feeding on the Lord's body and blood daily, it is sometimes hard to know precisely what they mean, which has led some scholars to see more eucharistic references in these texts than are actually there. Indeed, Augustine himself commented that the petition for daily bread in the Lord's Prayer could have different meanings: it could refer to material needs, to 'spiritual food', or to 'the sacrament of the body of Christ, which we receive daily' (*De sermone Domini in monte* 2.25); and in one of his sermons he speaks of the daily readings in church and of singing hymns, as well as the eucharist as being 'daily bread' (*Sermo* 57.7). In others he speaks of the word of God being daily bread to catechumens, and of Christ feeding them every day (*Sermones* 56.10; 132.1). Hence we need to be cautious whether apparent references to daily communion are to physical consumption or not, and indeed even if they are, how literally 'daily' is to be taken. So, for example, in a certain Abbot Isaac's discourse on prayer, does his exposition of the petition in the Lord's Prayer, 'Give us today our daily bread', refer to actual eating or not?

> For where it says 'daily' it shows that without it we cannot live a spiritual life for a single day. Where it says 'today' it shows that it must be received daily and that yesterday's supply of it is not enough, but that it must be given to us today also in like manner. And our daily need of it suggests to us that we ought at all times to offer up this prayer, because there is no day on which we have no need to strengthen the heart of our inner man, by eating and receiving it, although the expression used, 'today', may be taken to apply to this present life, i.e., while we are living in this world supply us with this bread.[12]

Other texts suggest that actual eucharistic practices among the monastic communities in the Egyptian desert varied. In some communities attendance at a eucharistic celebration appears to have been restricted to Sundays, and there is no indication of daily communion by individuals

---

[11] *De oratione* 19. For the precise nature of these gatherings, see Andrew B. McGowan, 'Rethinking Agape and Eucharist in Early North African Christianity', *Studia Liturgica* 34 (2004), pp. 165–76, here at p. 170.

[12] John Cassian, *Conferences* 9.21.

in their cells.[13] On the other hand, while the Rule of Pachomius refers only to this practice (*Praecepta* 15–16), other Pachomian sources describe as the normal custom both a Sunday eucharist celebrated in the monastery by a priest coming in from outside, and the monks also going to a near-by village for a Saturday evening *synaxis*.[14] Cassian similarly tells of the monks of lower Egypt assembling on both Saturdays and Sundays for communion 'at the third hour' but not otherwise leaving their cells (*De institutis coenobiorum* 3.2), as does the *Historia monachorum in Aegypto*.[15] The ecclesiastical historian Socrates adds an interesting detail about the form that the Saturday assemblies took among Christians in the region of Alexandria and Thebes: they 'do not participate in the mysteries in the manner usual among Christians in general: for after having eaten and satisfied themselves with food of all kinds, in the evening making their offerings they partake of the mysteries' (*Historia ecclesiastica* 5.22). This suggests that the association of the eucharist with a Sabbath evening meal may have continued here from earliest times, even after Sunday supplanted it elsewhere as the primary occasion for the celebration of the eucharist. The celebration of the eucharist on Saturdays as well as Sundays is very widely attested in the East in the fourth century, though not this particular form on the Saturday. Indeed, Saturday celebrations were so common that Socrates mistakenly believed that Alexandria and Rome, which had celebrations only on Sundays, must once have also had Saturday celebrations but 'on account of some ancient tradition, have ceased to do this'.[16]

At the same time, there is also evidence for the reception of communion every single day and not just Saturdays and Sundays among at least some of the desert fathers. Armand Veilleux insists that daily communion was not a feature of Pachomian monasticism,[17] but the *Historia monachorum*

---

[13] See Palladius, *Historia Lausica* 33.2 (where a priest and a deacon go to a community of women only on a Sunday); 59.2 (where a nun, Taor, does not go to the local church on Sunday with the rest of the community); and Daniel 7 in Benedicta Ward (ed.), *The Sayings of the Desert Fathers* (Mowbray, London 1975), p. 45. See also Jerome's account of monastic practices in Bethlehem (*Epistula* 108.20.3).

[14] See Armand Veilleux, *La liturgie dans le cénobitisme pachômien au quatrième siècle*, Studia Anselmiana 57 (Pontificium Institutum S. Anselmi, Rome 1968), pp. 228–32. He believes that the absence of any reference to a Saturday eucharist in the Rule can be explained by the fact that the section of the Rule that mentions the Sunday celebration is dealing with variations in the office on Sundays and feasts, and not specifically listing all the days on which the eucharist took place (pp. 233–4).

[15] 20.7; ET in Norman Russell, *The Lives of the Desert Fathers* (Mowbray, London 1981), p. 106.

[16] Socrates, *Historia ecclesiastica* 5.22. Athanasius, *Apologia contra Arianos* 11, confirms that Sunday was the only regular day for the eucharist in Alexandria.

[17] Veilleux, *La liturgie dans le cénobitisme pachômien au quatrième siècle*, p. 235.

in Aegypto describes the reception of communion at the ninth hour, before supper was eaten, as being a daily practice among some other desert ascetics, and strongly encourages it.[18] Cassian's *Conferences* also include references to the practice (7.30.2; 14.8.5), and it continued to be a feature of many later monastic traditions: the *Rule of the Master*, for example, prescribes daily communion of both bread and wine after None and before going into the refectory to eat (*Regula Magistri* 21–2).

Daily communion, however, was not merely a monastic practice. We know that the eucharist was celebrated only on Sundays at Rome in the fourth century, but in a letter written in 383 Jerome asserts that daily communion was practised there, apparently with both bread and wine, as he speaks of drinking as well as eating (*Epistula* 21.26–7); and in another letter written in 398 he says that it was the custom 'of the churches of Rome and Spain' (*Epistula* 71.6). Augustine was of the opinion that the majority of those who did not receive communion daily were 'in Eastern parts' (*De sermone Domini in monte* 2.26). There is also evidence that some would carry the eucharist with them on journeys for the purpose of daily communion, though it may also have been as a protection against the forces of evil.[19] Thus, in the sermon at the funeral of his brother Satyrus, Ambrose of Milan relates how Satyrus, even though he was not yet baptized and when the ship on which he was travelling was in danger of sinking, asked for the consecrated bread from some baptized companions, wrapped it in a cloth and fastened it round his neck before casting himself into the sea and so came safely to land (*De exitu fratris* 1.43). Although his intention was obviously apotropaic – to ward off the power of evil – yet it is probable that the others were carrying it primarily for the purpose of communion. Confirmation of this practice is provided by Palladius, who in his *Dialogue on the Life of St John Chrysostom*[20] tells of John receiving communion while on a journey. Whereas it is commonly assumed that bread alone would have been used for home communion and while travelling, it is worth noting that Jerome tells of a certain Exuperius, Bishop of Toulouse, who used to carry both bread and wine: 'his wicker basket contains the body of the Lord, and his plain glass-cup the precious blood' (*Epistula* 125.20). When this evidence is added to that

---

[18] 8.50–1, 56–7; ET in Russell, *The Lives of the Desert Fathers*, pp. 77–8, but note that his literal translation in note 12 (p. 131) conveys the accurate meaning of receiving communion rather than celebrating the eucharist. See also 2.7–8 (Russell, p. 64), where communion is received daily before the evening meal; but cf. 13.4, 8 (Russell, pp. 93–4), where a certain John is said to have eaten nothing except communion, which the priest brought him on Sundays.

[19] See below, p. 35.

[20] Ancient Christian Writers 45 (Newman Press, New York 1985), pp. 73, 189 n. 420.

of the *Apostolic Tradition* and to Jerome's remark about 'drinking' referred to earlier in this paragraph, it seems to confirm that in some places at least the tradition was for home communion to be in both kinds.

Daily celebration of the eucharist

The instances we have examined so far seem to be of communion from elements reserved from a Sunday celebration: this would necessarily have been so in the case of monastic communities in the desert and Christians on journeys, and appears to have been so for Rome and Spain too. In other cases, we have evidence for the celebration of the eucharist on some weekdays. Several fourth-century sources speak unambiguously of this, although there was obviously considerable variety from place to place, as Augustine notes: 'some receive daily the Body and Blood of the Lord, others receive it on certain days; in some places no day is omitted in the offering of the Holy Sacrifice; in others it is offered only on Saturday and Sunday, or even only on Sunday'.[21] In the West, weekday celebrations seem generally to have been limited to northern Italy and North Africa. Ambrose in Milan declares that the eucharist was celebrated there at midday on 'most days', but on fast days communion was received at the conclusion of the fast just before the evening meal (*Sermones in psalmum 118* 8.48; 18.28). In this latter case, it appears that the eucharist itself was not celebrated, and hence there was a reversion to what had presumably been the older custom. Is it possible that it was Ambrose himself who introduced more frequent celebration of the eucharist on other days? Daily eucharist also seems to have been a feature of North Africa in Augustine's day. Was that too something that Augustine imported from Milan, or simply a continuation of the trend towards more frequent celebrations of the eucharist that we see in Cyprian in the third century?[22]

As for the East, Chrysostom states that in Antioch 'on the Preparation [Friday], on the Sabbath, on the Lord's day, and on the day of martyrs, it is the same sacrifice that is performed' (*Homiliae in epistulam I ad Timotheum* 5.3). Egeria seems to know of the addition of a Wednesday eucharist at Jerusalem to the Friday, Saturday and Sunday pattern described by Chrysostom, except for Lent, when Wednesday and Friday reverted to being purely services of the word with the eucharist celebrated only on

---

[21] *Epistula* 54.2; ET from *Saint Augustine: Letters*, I, Fathers of the Church 12 (New York 1951), p. 253.

[22] For Cyprian, see above, p. 24; and for a thorough review of the evidence for daily celebrations of the eucharist in the West in the fourth century, see Daniel Callam, 'The Frequency of Mass in the Latin Church ca. 400', *Theological Studies* 45 (1984), pp. 613–50.

Saturdays and Sundays (*Itinerarium* 27.6), an arrangement also prescribed by canon 49 of the Council of Laodicea (*c.*383), while canon 51
directs that in the Lenten season the feasts of the martyrs also should not
be kept, but they should instead be commemorated on Saturdays and
Sundays. Alexandria, on the other had, seems to have retained a pure
service of the word on Wednesdays and Fridays throughout the year, for
Socrates not only declares that in that city the eucharist was celebrated
only on Sundays but also that on Wednesdays and Fridays 'the Scriptures
are read, and the doctors expound them; and all the usual services are
performed in their assemblies, except the celebration of the mysteries'
(*Historia ecclesiastica* 5.22).

To complete the picture, we need also to mention that towards the end
of the fourth century we encounter attempts to limit or even suppress
celebrations of the eucharist in private houses. Thus, while on one occasion Basil of Caesarea speaks of his allowing presbyters under interdict
to celebrate in private but not in public congregations (*Epistula* 199), in
his shorter monastic rule he forbids celebrations in houses except in
cases of extreme necessity (*Regulae brevius tractatae* 310). The Council of
Laodicea, canon 58, refused to allow either bishops or priests to celebrate
in houses, while the Second Council of Carthage (*c.*390), canon 9, allowed
presbyters to do so only with the permission of their bishop. Nevertheless, both the practice itself and also attempts to control it continued
in succeeding centuries, suggesting that it was a deep-seated and long-
established usage rather than a novelty of the period, and thus may be the
lingering remains of the domestic origins of Christian eucharistic meals.

Abstaining from communion: why did it occur?

For students of liturgical history who have been persuaded to abandon
the idea that the fourth century was some sort of golden age for
Christianity, there is the temptation to transfer that vision to an earlier
century: to regard the legitimization of Christianity under Constantine as
the turning-point when things began to decline and new converts were
allowed to enter the Church without careful scrutiny as to the depth of
their faith and dedication, while the faithful members in earlier generations had all been intensely committed to their beliefs and constantly maintained the highest levels of conduct. However, there are signs that this was
not always the case, especially with regard to regular attendance at Sunday
worship and participation in communion.

Already at the end of the second century Tertullian refers to some in
his region of North Africa who had scruples about receiving communion

on the weekly station days because they thought it would break their fast (*De oratione* 19). More seriously, the early-third-century Syrian *Didascalia Apostolorum* mentions that there are some who apparently prefer to go to the theatre rather than attend Sunday worship (2.59); and Origen also complains that some scarcely come to church even on feast days (*Homiliae in Genesim* 10.1). Furthermore, several years before the Peace of Constantine was established, the Synod of Elvira in Spain in 306 found it necessary to threaten with punishment those who absented themselves from church for three Sundays in succession (canon 21), while among the canons attributed to the Synod of Antioch in 341 but possibly belonging to an earlier synod in 330[23] is one that applied sanctions to those who attended church and listened to the ministry of the word but did not participate in prayer or communion with the rest (canon 2). This legislation recurs among the canons of later councils.

Evidence from the latter part of the fourth century reveals that by then, if not sooner, abstention from communion was not limited to a matter of weeks, but could last for months and even a year or more. Thus John Chrysostom in one of his homilies reveals that 'many partake of this sacrifice once in the whole year, others twice; others many times. Our word then is to all; not to those only who are here, but to those also who are settled in the desert. For they partake once in the year, and often indeed at intervals of two years.' He went on to indicate that, not surprisingly, those who communicated once a year generally did so at Easter, at the end of the forty-day fast of Lent:

> Tell me, I beseech thee, when after a year thou partakest of the Communion, dost thou think that the Forty Days are sufficient for thee for the purifying of the sins of all that time? And again, when a week has passed, dost thou give thyself up to the former things? Tell me now, if when thou hast been well for forty days after a long illness, thou shouldest again give thyself up to the food which caused the sickness, hast thou not lost thy former labour too? For if natural things are changed, much more those which depend on choice. As for instance, by nature we see, and naturally we have healthy eyes; but oftentimes from a bad habit [of body] our power of vision is injured. If then natural things are changed, much more those of choice. Thou assignest forty days for the health of the soul, or perhaps not even forty, and dost thou expect to propitiate God? Tell me, art thou in sport? These things I say, not as forbidding you the one and annual coming, but as wishing you to draw near continually.[24]

---

[23] See H. Hess, *The Canons of the Council of Sardica* (Clarendon Press, Oxford 1958), pp. 145–50, Appendix II, 'The Origins of the Canons of Antioch'.

[24] John Chrysostom, *Homiliae in epistulam ad Hebraeos* 17.7; ET from *NPNF*, First Series, 14:449.

As Chrysostom's reference to those 'who are settled in the desert' indicates, this lengthy abstention did not just involve lay people in the towns and cities but extended also to some who were leading eremitic and monastic lives in the desert. This is confirmed by the exhortation to receive the communion every Sunday that was addressed by a certain Abbot Theonas to some Egyptian monks who were apparently doing so only once a year:

> We ought not to suspend ourselves from the Lord's Communion because we confess ourselves sinners, but should more and more eagerly hasten to it for the healing of our soul, and purifying of our spirit, and seek there rather a remedy for our wounds with humility of mind and faith, as considering ourselves unworthy to receive so great grace. Otherwise we cannot worthily receive the Communion even once a year, as some do, who live in monasteries and so regard the dignity and holiness and value of the heavenly sacraments, as to think that none but saints and spotless persons should venture to receive them, and not rather that they would make us saints and pure by taking them. And these thereby fall into greater presumption and arrogance than what they seem to themselves to avoid, because at the time when they do receive them, they consider that they are worthy to receive them. But it is much better to receive them every Sunday for the healing of our infirmities, with that humility of heart, whereby we believe and confess that we can never touch those holy mysteries worthily, than to be puffed up by a foolish persuasion of heart, and believe that at the year's end we are worthy to receive them.[25]

On the other hand, there were other desert fathers who discouraged the reception of communion by monks whom they considered were in an unworthy spiritual state. The *Historia monachorum in Aegypto* tells of a certain priest called Eulogius, who is said to have received the gift of the knowledge of the spiritual state of each monk who approached the altar, and would instruct certain ones not to receive: 'Abstain for a while from the sacred Mysteries and repent with all your soul that you may win forgiveness for your sins and become worthy of the Communion of Christ. If you do not first purify your thoughts you may not approach the grace of God.' Another priest called Dioscorus would tell those who had 'pondered on the image of a woman during the night' not to approach the sacred mysteries.[26]

The practice of lengthy abstention from communion seems to have been more prevalent in the East than the West. Ambrose in Milan, in an

---

25 John Cassian, *Conferences* 23.21; ET from *NPNF*, Second Series, 11:531. For other instances of abstention from communion among desert ascetics, see also Palladius, *Historia Lausica* 17.9; 27.2; 59.2.

26 16.1–2; 20.1–2; ET from Russell, *The Lives of the Desert Fathers*, pp. 100, 105.

exposition of the Lord's Prayer to the newly baptized, describes it as being the custom of 'the Greeks in the East'. While this must surely be something of an exaggeration, it must have been sufficiently widespread there for him to think of it as such; but his inclusion of a warning about it in this address indicates that it was not unknown in Milan as well, and so might lead his hearers to imitate it: 'If bread is daily, why do you take it after a year, as the Greeks in the East are accustomed to do? Receive daily what is of benefit to you daily! So live that you may deserve to receive it daily! He who does not deserve to receive it daily does not deserve to receive it after a year.'[27] Augustine in Africa was rather more irenic in his approach to the issue. Having referred to those claiming that the eucharist was not to be received every day but only on days when one was living 'with greater purity and self-restraint', and also to those who took the opposite view, he claimed that both were honouring the Lord in their respective ways (*Epistula* 54.4). Yet, the fact that he even raised the matter suggests that it was an issue in his community. On the other hand, Jerome in Italy, while desiring those who had engaged in sexual intercourse to refrain from receiving communion at home, implies that abstention from communion in church for any reason was not common in Rome:

> The Apostle Paul tells us that when we have intercourse with our wives we cannot pray. If, then, sexual intercourse prevents what is less impor-tant – that is, prayer – how much more does it prevent what is more important – that is, the reception of the body of Christ? . . . I know that at Rome it is customary for the faithful always to receive the body of Christ, a custom which I neither censure nor indorse. 'Let every man be fully per-suaded in his own mind.' But I appeal to the consciences of those persons who after indulging in sexual intercourse on the same day receive the com-munion – having first, as Persius puts it, 'washed off the night in a flowing stream', and I ask such why they do not presume to approach the martyrs or to enter the churches. Is Christ of one mind abroad and of another at home? What is unlawful in church cannot be lawful at home.[28]

As the words of these various fourth-century figures reveal, the primary motivation for prolonged abstention from communion in most cases at this time seems to have been a sense of personal unworthiness rather than a lack of adequate commitment to the faith and practice of Chris-tianity, although there is some evidence for a general indifference towards

---

[27] Ambrose, *De sacramentis* 5.25; ET from *Saint Ambrose: Theological and Dogmatic Works*, Fathers of the Church 44 (Catholic University of America Press, Washington, DC 1963), p. 317.

[28] Jerome, *Epistula* 48.15; ET from *NPNF*, Second Series, 6:75.

liturgy among certain early adherents of the monastic movement that would no doubt have also contributed towards it.[29] But what gave rise among so many to this attitude of unworthiness to receive communion? The usual answer given by liturgical historians to this question is that preachers like Chrysostom instilled it in them by insisting on the necessity of purity of conscience in order to approach the eucharistic table. And certainly he does attack those who appear to him to have a casual attitude towards the reception of communion and receive it at specific holy seasons regardless of the state of their soul:

> I observe many partaking of Christ's body lightly and just as it happens, and rather from custom and form than consideration and understanding. When, saith a man, the holy season of Lent sets in, whatever a man may be, he partakes of the mysteries, or, when the day of the Lord's Epiphany comes. And yet it is not the Epiphany, nor is it Lent, that makes a fit time for approaching, but it is sincerity and purity of soul. With this, approach at all times; without it, never.[30]

However, it appears that these same people were already abstaining from communion at other times of the year:

> At the other times ye come not, no, not though often ye are clean; but at Easter, however flagrant an act ye may have committed, ye come. Oh! the force of custom and of prejudice! In vain is the daily Sacrifice, in vain do we stand before the Altar; there is no one to partake. These things I am saying, not to induce you to partake anyhow, but that ye should render yourselves worthy to partake.

He went on to urge them, if they were not intending to receive communion, to leave the eucharistic assembly after the ministry of the word – in effect, to return to the status of catechumens – because if they were unworthy to receive communion, they were equally unworthy to join in the prayers of the faithful:

> As then it is not meet that any one of the uninitiated be present, so neither is it that one of them that are initiated, and yet at the same time defiled. Tell me, suppose any one were invited to a feast, and were to wash his hands, and sit down, and be all ready at the table, and after all refuse to partake; is he not insulting the man who invited him? Were it

---

[29] See Robert F. Taft, 'Home Communion in the Late Antique East', in Clare V. Johnson (ed.), *Ars Liturgiae: Worship, Aesthetics, and Praxis: Essays in Honor of Nathan D. Mitchell* (Liturgy Training Publications, Chicago 2003), pp. 1–15, here at pp. 4–7.

[30] *Homiliae in epistulam ad Ephesios* 3.4; ET from *NPNF*, First Series, 13:63. See also *Homiliae in epistulam I ad Corinthios* 28.1.

not better for such an one never to have come at all? Now it is just in the same way that thou hast come here. Thou hast sung the hymn with the rest: thou hast declared thyself to be of the number of them that are worthy, by not departing with them that are unworthy. Why stay, and yet not partake of the table? I am unworthy, thou wilt say. Then art thou also unworthy of that communion thou hast had in prayers.[31]

Chrysostom repeated in other homilies the message of the need for worthiness before receiving communion:

What then? Which shall we approve? Those [who receive] once [in the year]? Those who [receive] many times? Those who [receive] few times? Neither those [who receive] once, nor those [who receive] often, nor those [who receive] seldom, but those [who come] with a pure conscience, from a pure heart, with an irreproachable life. Let such draw near continually; but those who are not such, not even once. Why, you will ask? Because they receive to themselves judgment, yea and condemnation, and punishment, and vengeance.[32]

In another homily he spelled out more fully the consequences of unworthy reception:

Since the Priests cannot know who are sinners, and unworthy partakers of the holy Mysteries, God often in this way delivers them to Satan. For when diseases, and attacks, and sorrows, and calamities, and the like occur, it is on this account that they are inflicted. This is shown by Paul. 'For this cause many are weak and sickly among you, and many sleep' [1 Cor. 11:30]. But how? saith one, when we approach but once a year! But this is indeed the evil, that you determine the worthiness of your approach, not by the purity of your minds, but by the interval of time. You think it a proper caution not to communicate often; not considering that you are seared by partaking unworthily, though only once, but to receive worthily, though often, is salutary. It is not presumptuous to receive often, but to receive unworthily, though but once in a whole life.[33]

And he insisted that those who administered communion were also responsible for ensuring that the unworthy did not receive:

These things I say to you that receive, and to you that minister. For it is necessary to address myself to you also, that you may with much care

---

[31] *Homiliae in epistulam ad Ephesios* 3.4; ET from *NPNF*, First Series, 13:64. It is interesting to observe that a parallel argument against non-communicants remaining in church while others received communion was also advanced in the first exhortation included in the eucharistic rite of the 1552 *Book of Common Prayer* of the Church of England.

[32] *Homiliae in epistulam ad Hebraeos* 17.7; ET from *NPNF*, First Series, 14:449.

[33] *Homiliae in epistulam I ad Timotheum* 5.3; ET from *NPNF*, First Series, 13:425.

distribute the gifts there. There is no small punishment for you, if being conscious of any wickedness in any man, you allow him to partake of this table. 'His blood shall be required at your hands.' Though any one be a general, though a deputy, though it be he himself who is invested with the diadem, and come unworthily, forbid him, the authority thou hast is greater than his. Thou, if thou wert entrusted to keep a spring of water clean for a flock, and then wert to see a sheep having much mire on its mouth, thou wouldest not suffer it to stoop down unto it and foul the stream: but now being entrusted with a spring not of water, but of blood and of spirit, if thou seest any having on them sin, which is more grievous than earth and mire, coming unto it, art thou not displeased? Dost thou not drive them off? And what excuse canst thou have? For this end God hath honoured you with this honour, that ye should discern these things. This is your office, this your safety, this your whole crown, not that ye should go about clothed in a white and shining vestment.[34]

As the above quotations indicate, while Chrysostom certainly desired more frequent reception of communion, he neither approved nor condemned those who abstained. That was not his primary focus, but, like certain of the desert fathers cited earlier, he was much more concerned to prevent unworthy reception whenever that might occur. The quotations also imply that infrequent reception was already a long-established custom in his day, and not something brought about by his preaching. Many of those against whom he was directing his strictures were already abstaining from communion, and Chrysostom was focusing his attention on the occasions on which they did decide to communicate, because he thought that they were still unworthy to do so. We need to search elsewhere, then, for the original causes of this phenomenon. Although a definitive answer is not immediately obvious, the following factors need to be noted:

- Absence from church by some on Sundays was already occurring before the Peace of Constantine, according to the evidence cited earlier in this chapter, but in so far as we can discern a reason for it at this time, it seems to have been lack of commitment rather than a sense of unworthiness.
- Prior to the fourth century those living deep in the countryside would often have been unable to attend the eucharist every Sunday, unlike those in towns and cities, because of the distances involved. Did this encourage an expectation that less frequent attendance or participation in communion was acceptable?

---

[34] *Homiliae in Matthaeum* 82.6; ET from *NPNF*, First Series, 10:477.

- Many of the new converts after the Peace of Constantine would not have been accustomed to a religion that expected such intimate involvement in its rites on a weekly basis and the need for constant purity that accompanied it. Was it among them that the sense of unworthiness to receive communion frequently arose?

- While some of the fourth-century desert ascetics were practising daily communion, others were being discouraged from receiving the sacrament at all if they were in an unworthy spiritual state. As the flight to the desert was often marked by a heightened awareness of human sinfulness, is it possible that prolonged abstinence from communion first arose there as a result of that attitude and then spread elsewhere?

- The generally observed prohibition on fasting or kneeling for prayer on Sundays, first reported by Tertullian (*De corona* 3; *De oratione* 23), meant that penitential prayer in preparation for the reception of communion was not possible within the eucharistic rite itself.[35] Did this absence of a means to purify oneself at the time of reception also help to discourage some from communion?

- Could the notion that the consecrated bread and wine had power to protect or heal without the need to consume them have also played a part? Third-century sources reveal the existence in a belief in the apotropaic power of the eucharist when consumed,[36] and fourth-century sources extend this idea, referring both to its application to parts of the body in connection with its consumption,[37] and also to its healing power when applied to an infection or wound without consuming it.[38]

---

[35] The only penitential reference in many eucharistic rites until several centuries later was the Lord's Prayer, with its petition for forgiveness, which makes its first appearance in some, but apparently not all, eucharistic rites in the second half of the fourth century: see Robert F. Taft, 'The Lord's Prayer in the Eucharistic Liturgy: When and Why?', *Ecclesia Orans* 14 (1997), pp. 137–55, esp. p. 153, and below, pp. 132–44.

[36] See Cyprian, *Epistula* 57.2; *Apostolic Tradition* 36.

[37] 'Then having carefully sanctified the eyes with a touch of the holy body, consume, taking heed not to drop any of it . . . Then after partaking of Christ's body, come also to the cup of the blood, not stretching out the hands but bowing and saying *Amen* in the manner of worship and reverence, sanctify yourself also by partaking of Christ's blood. And while the moisture is still on the lips, touching it with your hands, sanctify both the eyes and forehead and the other organs of sense' (*Mystagogical Catecheses* attributed to Cyril of Jerusalem, 5.21–2); Theodore of Mopsuestia: 'When you have received the body in your hands, you adore it . . . With a great and sincere love you place it on your eyes, kiss it and address to it your prayers as to Christ our Lord . . .' (*Baptismal Homily* 5.28; ET from *AIR*, p. 242).

[38] Augustine, *Contra Iulianum* 3.162; Gregory Nazianzus, *Oratio* 8.18. See also Ambrose's account of his brother Satyrus carrying the eucharistic bread around his neck for protection against evil (*De exitu fratris* 1.43), above, p. 26.

Conclusion: a communion-centred eucharistic piety

The cumulative effect of the practices outlined above – the early adoption
of weekday communion at home, the taking of the sacrament to those unable to be present, the eventual multiplication of opportunities to receive
communion at church during the week, whether in a distribution of
previously consecrated elements or in a full eucharist – is to suggest that,
while 'official' eucharistic theology, the theology of church leaders, may
have centred on the importance of the congregation of believers offering the sacrifice of praise together in the celebration, the actual piety of
ordinary Christians may have been shaped more by a focus on communion, on feeding on Christ. Whether this was done alone or with others,
at a eucharist or outside it, may have seemed relatively inconsequential to
them – just as the fundamental needs of the poor had been to have their
hunger satisfied, and whether this was to be done at the supper or by
the reception of leftovers was of much less importance than the reception
of the food itself. It is also worth noting that in much pagan sacrifice
central importance was accorded to the worshippers' participation in the
consumption of the sacrificial victim and not in their presence at or
assistance with its offering as such, and this would have formed the
background piety of many converts to Christianity. Even the prolonged
abstention from communion by some is a sign of the significance that
was being attached to its reception at the time, in spite of the fact that
in the long term it contributed to the view that the communion of all
the faithful was a dispensable element in the offering of the eucharistic
sacrifice. Indeed, if it is correct to interpret a statement by Innocent I in
his letter to Decentius at the beginning of the fifth century as denoting
the existence in the *tituli* churches of Rome on Sundays of services of the
word accompanied by the distribution of communion consecrated by
bread brought from the papal celebration rather than independent
eucharists, then communion divorced from consecration formed the
normal eucharistic experience for the majority of Roman Christians for
a good many years.[39]

These ancient precedents, however, should not be treated as constituting legitimate justification for continuing such present-day practices as
regularly dispensing communion from the reserved sacrament rather
than from elements consecrated at the time or for importing previously
consecrated bread and wine from another eucharistic community when

---

[39] See John F. Baldovin, 'The Fermentum at Rome in the Fifth Century: A Reconsideration',
Worship 79 (2005), pp. 38–53.

the absence of a priest makes a full eucharistic celebration in one community impossible. Early Christians were just as capable of theological and liturgical distortions as their modern counterparts; and there are signs to suggest that some of them at least may have been aware of the dangers of such a communion-centred piety. Whether for this reason, or simply because of a desire to curb a practice that was not subject to ecclesiastical control and so could allow Arians to receive communion, the Council of Saragossa (379–81), canon 3, and the Council of Toledo (400), canon 14, tried to prevent the sacrament from being taken home. Similarly, Leo the Great in Rome in the fifth century seems to have preferred to have more than one celebration of the eucharist in a church on greater festivals as a lesser evil than the people being deprived of their opportunity to participate in the oblation:

> when any of the greater festivals has brought together a larger congregation than usual, and too great a crowd of the faithful has assembled for one church to hold them all at once, there should be no hesitation about repeating the oblation of the sacrifice: lest, if those only are admitted to this service who come first, those who flock in afterwards should seem to. be rejected: for it is fully in accordance with piety and reason, that as often as a fresh congregation has filled the church where service is going on, the sacrifice should be offered as a matter of course. Whereas a certain portion of the people must be deprived of their worship, if the custom of only one celebration be kept, and only those who come early in the day can offer the sacrifice.[40]

---

[40] *Epistula* 9.3; ET from *NPNF*, Second Series, 12:8.

3

The earliest eucharistic prayers?

Because of the shortage of other substantial evidence for the form that early eucharistic prayers would have taken, two liturgical texts – the meal prayers in the *Didache* and the eucharistic prayer in the so-called *Apostolic Tradition of Hippolytus* – have come to assume a position of crucial importance in attempts that have been made to reconstruct the line of development of such prayers from the earliest times down to the fourth century, when more examples of eucharistic anaphoras become visible. Unfortunately, both these texts present problems of interpretation and have often been wrongly used to support inaccurate conclusions.

The scholarly consensus that emerged during the course of the twentieth century was that Christian eucharistic prayers had developed out of the Jewish grace after meals, the *Birkat ha-mazon*. This was in spite of the fact that a growing number of Jewish scholars began to express doubts as to whether such prayers would have existed in the first century in the fixed form in which they are later found,[1] and also despite the fact that in Jewish tradition that particular prayer came to mark the point in the meal after which no further food could be consumed, although wine might still be drunk.[2] Enrico Mazza was a partial exception to this consensus. Although still seeing some eucharistic prayers as emanating from the grace after meals, he traced the roots of the eucharistic prayer in the fourth-century *Apostolic Constitutions* 7 through its source in the *Didache* to the short Jewish blessings over cup and bread that would have been

[1] Among recent contributions see, for example, Stefan C. Reif, 'The Second Temple Period, Qumran Research, and Rabbinic Liturgy: Some Contextual and Linguistic Comparisons', in Esther G. Chazon (ed.), *Liturgical Perspectives: Prayer and Poetry in Light of the Dead Sea Scrolls* (Brill, Leiden 2003), pp. 133–49; and Richard S. Sarason, 'Communal Prayer at Qumran and Among the Rabbis: Certainties and Uncertainties', in ibid., pp. 151–72.

[2] See Clemens Leonhard, 'Blessings over Wine and Bread in Judaism and Christian Eucharistic Prayers: Two Independent Traditions', in Albert Gerhards and Clemens Leonhard (eds), *Jewish and Christian Liturgy and Worship: New Insights into its History and Interaction* (Brill, Leiden 2007), pp. 309–26. Leonhard also makes the point that the rabbinic *berakah* releases food from its sacred character and makes it available to eat, while the Christian prayer on the contrary makes sacred what was formerly profane food.

used earlier in the meal, and he proposed that the *Yotzer,* one of the blessings before the *Shema* in Jewish morning prayer, was the ultimate source of the eucharistic prayer of the Strasbourg Papyrus.[3] Yet there is no reason to suppose that these other Jewish texts existed in a definitive form at such an early date any more than the grace after meals did, nor that the early Christians would have cast around for an already existing prayer from a quite different liturgical context – morning prayer – to use as a model for their praying over their meal rather than develop one themselves. In any case, very few later Christian eucharistic texts show any obvious influence of Jewish antecedents, however hard some scholars have tried to find them there. However, let us start with those that do. Chief among these are the meal prayers in the *Didache.*

Didache 9–10

9.1 *Concerning the thanksgiving, give thanks thus:*

  2 *First, concerning the cup:*

    We give thanks to you, our Father, for the holy vine of David your child, which you have made known to us through Jesus your child; glory to you for evermore.

  3 *Concerning the broken bread:*

    We give thanks to you, our Father, for the life and knowledge which you have made known to us through Jesus your child; glory to you for evermore.

  4 As this broken bread was scattered upon the mountains and having been gathered together became one, so may your church be gathered together from the ends of the earth into your kingdom; for yours is the glory and the power through Jesus Christ for evermore.

  5 *Let no one eat or drink of your eucharist but those who have been baptized in the name of the Lord. For concerning this also the Lord has said, 'Do not give what is holy to the dogs.'*

10.1 *After you have had your fill, give thanks thus:*

  2 We give thanks to you, holy Father, for your holy name which you have enshrined in our hearts, and for the knowledge and faith and immortality which you have made known to us through Jesus your child; glory to you for evermore.

---

[3] Enrico Mazza, *The Origins of the Eucharistic Prayer* (The Liturgical Press, Collegeville 1995), pp. 12–61, 194–6.

3 You, Almighty Master, created all things for the sake of your Name and gave food and drink to humans for enjoyment, that they might give thanks to you; but to us you have granted spiritual food and drink and eternal life through Jesus your child.

4 Above all we give thanks to you because you are mighty; glory to you for evermore. Amen.

5 Remember, Lord, your church, to deliver it from all evil and to perfect it in your love, and gather it together from the four winds, having been sanctified, into your kingdom which you have prepared for it; for yours is the power and the glory for evermore. Amen.

6 May grace come, and this world pass away. Amen.
Hosanna to the God of David.
If anyone is holy, let him come; if anyone is not, let him repent.
Marana tha. Amen.

7 *But allow the prophets to give thanks as they wish.*

Although in the past many scholars tried to exclude these prayers from consideration on the grounds that they did not resemble later eucharistic prayers, and especially because they lacked a narrative of the Last Supper, and so this meal cannot have been a eucharist as such,[4] the tide has turned among liturgical historians, and the majority now do regard it as an early form of the eucharist. Yet that does not solve all the problems related to the material. Providing an explanation that does justice to all of its significant features is an extremely difficult task, which is why so many different theories about it can still abound. One recent commentator on the text, Alan Garrow, has likened it to trying to cover all four corners of a mattress with an insufficiently large fitted sheet.[5] Any who have struggled to make such a bed will readily understand his comparison: it is often possible to get the sheet to cover three corners, but the fourth can only be managed at the expense of one of the others. What we might call the 'awkward corners' of the *Didache* text are chiefly as follows:

- the fact that 10.1 speaks of having just completed a full meal, while 10.6 appears, at least to some scholars, to include an invitation to receive communion after the meal, creates difficulties for those who want to see the meal itself as eucharistic;

---

[4] For further details, see Bradshaw, *Eucharistic Origins*, pp. 25–30.
[5] Alan Garrow, *The Gospel of Matthew's Dependence on the Didache* (T & T Clark, London/New York 2004), p. 14.

- on the other hand, the restriction of the eucharist to the baptized in 9.5 appears to contradict this and imply that the meal is eucharistic;
- similarly, the use of the word *klasma*, 'broken piece', in 9.3 and 9.4 rather than *artos*, 'bread', is perhaps suggestive that the meal is eucharistic, but it appears to imply that the bread has already been broken before the prayer rather than after it, which is odd;
- and finally, the fact that the prayers in both 9 and 10 have strong parallels to one another and both seem to be eucharistic in character makes it difficult to regard one set as related to an 'ordinary meal' and the other not, and yet there cannot be two eucharists here, can there?

Garrow's own solution to these difficulties is to propose that there are in fact two parallel liturgies, one comprising chapter 9 and the other chapter 10, and that 'they represent two separate accounts of the same liturgical event'.[6] He draws particular attention to the parallels in structure and contents between the two sets of prayers. He believes that in each case a full meal would have preceded the prayers, which is indicated by the rubric in 10.1 and implied by the use of *klasma* in chapter 9, referring to a large piece of the loaf which would have been broken at the beginning of the meal before these prayers. In both cases, then, the prayers refer forwards to the eucharistic communion that is to follow, indicated in the one case by the direction in 9.5 about who may receive communion, and in the other case by the invitation in 10.6, which also refers to those who may and may not receive. He concludes that these two chapters belong to separate layers of tradition, and were juxtaposed in the compilation of the *Didache* only because of their common subject matter.

Garrow may have hit upon something close to the right answer. The striking similarities in both structure and content of the two sets of prayers which he has emphasized do seem to point towards their being alternative outworkings from the same root tradition, those in chapter 9 representing a more primitive version of the material with the units over cup and bread still being clearly differentiated from one another, while in chapter 10 it has been moulded into a more continuous whole. Garrow's hypothesis thus helps solve another puzzling feature of the text which has commonly been ignored by scholars – how it could be that a single meal ritual could include prayers that were nearly duplicates of one another in both form and content. While there is certainly no shortage of historical examples of liturgies that contain alternative versions of the

---

[6] Ibid., p. 25.

same material within the one rite, this is nearly always the result of the fusion of what had earlier been quite discrete and parallel texts rather than the work of a single compiler.

However, I would want to modify Garrow's view somewhat. He assumes (a) that the prayer material in these chapters reached the compiler of the *Didache* complete with the accompanying directions; (b) that the rite was then still in actual liturgical use; and (c) that the compiler juxtaposed the parallel sets of prayers merely because of their commonality of subject. All these assumptions are questionable. First, early liturgical prayers seem to have been commonly transmitted without any accompanying directions as to their precise use or location within a rite. Thus, for example, in the earliest-known collection of Christian liturgical prayers, the mid-fourth-century *Sacramentary of Sarapion*, most prayers have only a very general title attached to them (such as 'Prayer for Those being Baptized' or 'Prayer for One Who Has Died and is Being Carried Out').[7] In the light of this, it seems probable that the prayers themselves in *Didache* 9 and 10 were at first in oral circulation and were received by the compiler with little, if any, indication as to their exact location within the ritual meal. Second, there is no reason to suppose that when the compiler did acquire these prayers, they were in current use; indeed, since it was not usual to write down prayers at that time, the primary reason for doing so and including them within the church order was very probably that they were becoming obsolete and in danger of being forgotten. Third, there is again no reason to suppose that the compiler viewed them as two alternative sets of prayers for the Christian meal, even though that was apparently what they were, but it is at least just as likely that he understood them to belong to the one ritual.

However, if they had no accompanying directions, except probably for what became 9.5 (which is of a different sort – a community rule rather than an instruction about a liturgical action), how should they be arranged? Which set should come first and which second? Let us imagine the situation of the compiler. The prayer in 9.2, with its reference to the holy vine of David, appeared to be intended as a prayer over wine, and so he prefaced it with the directions: 'Concerning the thanksgiving, give thanks thus: First, concerning the cup'. The second unit with thanksgiving and petition mentioned broken bread, *klasma*, and so the compiler inserted before it, 'And concerning the fragment (*peri tou klasmatou*)', rather

---

[7] See Johnson, *The Prayers of Sarapion of Thmuis*, pp. 55, 69.

than 'And concerning the bread (*peri tou artou*)'.[8] But what should he then do with the material we know as chapter 10, without any accompanying rubrical assistance and merely a more general reference to spiritual food and drink in the text? Since he already had prayers for use over cup and bread before the meal, he concluded that it must have been intended for use after the meal was over, and so inserted the direction, 'After you have had your fill, give thanks thus', and left it at that.

In short, what I am proposing is that, while the prayer material in chapters 9 and 10 may well be very ancient and authentic, its layout in the *Didache* is later and completely artificial and so tells us nothing at all about the structure of primitive eucharistic celebrations. It certainly does not require us to think that the meal must have been eaten before prayers over the cup and bread were said and the eucharistic elements distributed, for once the direction in 10.1 is eliminated, the presence or absence of a meal either before or after the prayers becomes an entirely open question. Nonetheless, understanding the material as composed of two parallel variants of the same liturgical tradition does enable us to glimpse two distinct stages in the evolution of eucharistic prayers, from separate prayers over cup and bread in chapter 9 to a single prayer over both in chapter 10, with no indication there of any temporal priority of cup over bread or of bread over cup. The hypothesis that the contents of chapters 9 and 10 circulated independently of one another may also help explain the presence of some material paralleling chapter 9 but not accompanied by any material from chapter 10 in two later texts, in the eucharistic prayer of the *Sacramentary of Sarapion* and in the grace at table for a religious community of women in the anonymous *De virginitate*, formerly but wrongly attributed to Athanasius.[9] Above all, it resolves

---

[8] The word *klasma* appears to be used proleptically here, but it has been suggested that it is perhaps also influenced by knowledge of a version of the story of the Feeding of the Five Thousand in John 6.1–15, where there is reference in verse 12 to 'fragments' being 'gathered', which may be intended symbolically of the gathering of Christian disciples 'that nothing may be lost', see C. F. D. Moule, 'A Note on *Didache* ix.4', *Journal of Theological Studies* 6 (1955), pp. 240–3; Francis J. Moloney, *The Gospel of John* (The Liturgical Press, Collegeville 1998), pp. 198–200. An alternative possibility, which does not seem to have been considered, is that the breaking of the bread may actually have been intended to precede the saying of the prayer. Although this sequence is not otherwise recorded in either Jewish or early Christian sources, it would not be dissimilar from other variations in the order of ritual actions that we do encounter in different groups of both Christians (e.g., bread/cup or cup/bread) and rabbinic Jews (e.g., the debates in the Mishnah tractate *Berakoth* over the order that certain blessings were to be said). In addition, we should note that *Didache* 14.1 has the identical order: 'break bread and give thanks'.

[9] See further Bradshaw, *Eucharistic Origins*, pp. 116–21.

nearly all the difficulties associated with other theories, and so is worth taking seriously as an explanation for this puzzling but crucial text in the early history of eucharistic rites.

A different trajectory

Whatever the true origin and nature of the material in *Didache* 9–10, what is clear is that, while it is certainly Jewish in character, for the reasons outlined at the beginning of the chapter it cannot simply be described as an adaptation of existing Jewish texts but should rather be seen as a natural development within a Jewish-Christian milieu.[10] When one turns to other early eucharistic prayers, however, there are very few indeed that have survived that retain a similar Semitic style. First, there are three fourth-century texts that exhibit a literary relationship with the *Didache* material – the prayer in *Apostolic Constitutions* 7 mentioned by Mazza and referred to at the beginning of this chapter, together with the two instances mentioned above, the middle of the eucharistic prayer of the *Sacramentary of Sarapion* and *De virginitate* 12–13. Taken together, these three texts seem to point to the conclusion that the kind of prayers found in *Didache* 9–10 continued to be used at least within certain limited segments of early Christianity for a considerable number of years, but apparently eventually faded away.

Equally striking in its resemblance to Jewish patterns of praying is the Anaphora of Addai and Mari, composed in Syriac rather than Greek, the core of which must go back at least to the fourth century and very probably much earlier still.[11] Although some scholars have claimed to see parallels in it to the tripartite Jewish grace after meals,[12] and others to the bipartite morning prayers said before the *Shema* each day,[13] there are enough

---

[10] For a more detailed study of this material, see ibid., pp. 32–9.

[11] For a critical edition, see William Macomber, 'The Oldest Known Text of the Anaphora of the Apostles Addai and Mari', *Orientalia Christiana Periodica* 31 (1966), pp. 335–71; for an ET of the text and bibliography of secondary literature, see Bryan D. Spinks (ed.), *Addai and Mari – The Anaphora of the Apostles: A Text for Students*, Grove Liturgical Study 24 (Grove Books, Nottingham 1980); and Anthony Gelston, *The Eucharistic Prayer of Addai and Mari* (Clarendon Press, Oxford 1992).

[12] See, for example, Gerard Rouwhorst, 'Jewish Liturgical Traditions in Early Syriac Christianity', *Vigiliae Christianae* 51 (1997), pp. 72–93, here at pp. 79–80.

[13] See, for example, Jacob Vellian, 'The Anaphoral Structure of Addai and Mari compared to the Berakoth Preceding the Shema in the Synagogue Morning Service contained in Seder R. Amram Gaon', *Le Muséon* 85 (1972), pp. 201–23; Bryan D. Spinks, 'The Original Form of the Anaphora of the Apostles: A Suggestion in the Light of Maronite *Sharar*', *Ephemerides Liturgicae* 91 (1977), pp. 146–61 = idem, *Worship: Prayers from the East* (Pastoral Press, Washington, DC 1993), pp. 21–36.

significant differences from both these texts that render it extremely improbable that either of them constitutes the primary source for this prayer.[14] Nonetheless, the similarities that do exist seem to confirm its roots as having been in a Jewish-Christian context.

Yet such texts are the exception rather than the rule among the extant eucharistic prayers that are known from the fourth century onwards. The majority seem rather to have left their Jewish roots behind and taken a different trajectory. There are some signs that at first in some communities separate prayers may have continued to be said over bread and cup, as they were in *Didache* 9, rather than in a united form, as may have been the case with the prayer in *Didache* 10. Thus Justin Martyr in the second century uses the plural when describing what the president does (he 'sends up prayer*s* and thanksgiving*s* to the best of his ability': *First Apology* 67.4) and the third-century Syrian *Didascalia* suggests that a visiting bishop might be invited to 'speak the words over the cup'.[15] There are also signs that some prayers may have been created by combining together originally separate units, as were their Jewish antecedents, rather than as continuous through compositions.[16] And of course they all continue to offer praise, just as the Jewish meal prayers had done. But their style is quite different, and the prayers are described by authors from the late second century onwards as being an 'invocation' (*epiklesis*), suggesting that the emphasis was seen as falling more on their petitionary aspect than on the *eucharistia* alone. Indeed, that word came instead to refer to the eucharistic elements, and especially the bread.[17] Before looking further at these later texts, however, we need first to deal with one prayer that conventionally has been thought to date from the early third century and to be typical of eucharistic praying in general at that period, a conclusion that thus greatly affected how early anaphoras were understood to have developed.

The eucharistic prayer in the so-called *Apostolic Tradition* of Hippolytus

4.3 The Lord [be] with you.
And let them all say: And with your spirit.
Up [with your] hearts.

---

[14] For further discussion, see Bradshaw, *Eucharistic Origins*, pp. 128–31.
[15] *Didascalia Apostolorum* 2.57. For further discussion of both these passages, see Bradshaw, *Eucharistic Origins*, pp. 75, 104–5.
[16] Ibid., pp. 121–3.
[17] See for example, Justin Martyr, *First Apology* 66.1.

We have [them] to the Lord.

Let us give thanks to the Lord.

It is worthy and just.

And so let him then continue:

4 We render thanks to you, God, through your beloved child Jesus Christ, whom in the last times you sent to us as savior and redeemer and angel of your will,

5 who is your inseparable word, through whom you made all things and it was well pleasing to you,

6 [whom] you sent from heaven into the virgin's womb, and who conceived in the womb was incarnate and manifested as your Son, born from the Holy Spirit and the virgin;

7 who fulfilling your will and gaining for you a holy people stretched out [his] hands when he was suffering, that he might release from suffering those who believed in you;

8 who when he was being handed over to voluntary suffering, that he might destroy death and break the bonds of the devil, and tread down hell and the illuminate the righteous, and fix a limit and manifest the resurrection,

9 taking bread [and] giving thanks to you, he said: 'Take, eat, this is my body that will be broken for you.' Likewise also the cup, saying, 'This is my blood that is shed for you.

10 When you do this, you do my remembrance.'

11 Remembering therefore his death and resurrection, we offer to you the bread and cup, giving thanks to you because you have held us worthy to stand before you and minister to you.

12 And we ask that you would send your Holy Spirit in the oblation of [your] holy church, [that] gathering [them] into one you will give to all who partake of the holy things [to partake] in the fullness of the Holy Spirit, for the strengthening of faith in truth,

13 that we may praise and glorify you through your child Jesus Christ, through whom [be] glory and honor to you, Father and Son with the Holy Spirit, in your holy church, both now and to the ages of ages. Amen.[18]

Among the manuscripts of ancient church orders discovered by scholars during the nineteenth century was one that, because it was anonymous

---

[18] *Apostolic Tradition* 4 (Latin version); ET from Bradshaw, Johnson, and Phillips, *The Apostolic Tradition: A Commentary*, pp. 38–40.

and untitled, was given the name 'The Egyptian Church Order' by Hans Achelis in 1891, since up to that date all the linguistic versions in which it had been found had belonged to that part of the world – two dialects of Coptic (Sahidic and Bohairic) and Ethiopic. In 1900, however, Edmund Hauler published an incomplete fifth-century Latin text of it, and four years later George Horner added an Arabic version to the collection. Although it was agreed that the original behind all these versions had been written in Greek, only a few fragments of the text in that language have ever been discovered.

It was in 1906 that Eduard von der Goltz came up with the suggestion that it might in reality be a work by Hippolytus of Rome, the *Apostolic Tradition*, previously believed to have been lost,[19] and this theory was then taken up and elaborated, first by Eduard Schwartz in 1910, and then quite independently and much more fully by R. H. Connolly in 1916.[20] This verdict was subsequently accepted by the great majority of scholars and the church order was commonly assumed to represent the official liturgy of the Church at Rome in the early third century. Because, apart from the *Didache*, there were no other extant texts containing liturgical material that could be attributed with any certainty to such an early date, and because it was thought to reflect the practice of such a major centre of ancient Christianity, it came to play a crucial role not only in scholarly reconstructions of primitive Christian worship practices but also in the process of liturgical revision undertaken in many mainstream Christian denominations in the second half of the twentieth century. Out of a desire to restore in modern practice elements of early Christian worship that had been lost or at least diminished in later liturgical traditions, parts of this church order, and especially its eucharistic prayer, were copied and adapted in many new rites that were being composed and authorized for use at this time.

The attribution to Hippolytus rested mainly upon two principal foundations. The first was that, while no existing manuscript of the document itself bore a title or author's name, two other church orders derived from

---

[19] Eduard von der Goltz, 'Unbekannte Fragmente altchristlicher Gemeindeordnungen', *Sitzungsberichte der Preussischen Akademie der Wissenschaften* (1906), pp. 141–57; see also idem, 'Die Taufgebete Hippolyts und andere Taufgebete der alten Kirchen', *Zeitschrift für Kirchengeschichte* 27 (1906), pp. 1–51.

[20] Eduard Schwartz, *Uber die pseudoapostolischen Kirchenordnungen* (Trubner, Strasbourg 1910) = idem, *Gesammelte Schriften* 5 (de Gruyter, Berlin 1963), pp. 192–273; Richard H. Connolly, *The So-called Egyptian Church Order and Derived Documents* (Cambridge University Press, Cambridge 1916 = Kraus, Nendeln, Liechtenstein 1967).

it do make reference to Hippolytus. One is actually entitled *The Canons of Hippolytus*, and the other – the *Epitome* of *Apostolic Constitutions* Book 8 – introduces a subheading, 'Constitutions of the Holy Apostles concerning Ordinations through Hippolytus', at precisely the point where it begins to draw directly upon a text of the document rather than upon *Apostolic Constitutions* Book 8 itself. The second argument was that both the prologue and epilogue of the work apparently use the expression 'apostolic tradition'. That there had once been a work by Hippolytus called 'The Apostolic Tradition' seemed to be proved by its inclusion in a list of titles of writings inscribed on the right-hand side of the base of a statue discovered in Rome in 1551, most of which were known to have Hippolytus as their author.

Although there had always been a few scholars who had doubted the veracity of the consensus that had been reached with regard to the identity of the document, it was not until about twenty years ago – long after modern versions of the material had become established parts of contemporary service-books – that their number began to grow and their arguments were taken seriously by an ever-widening circle of liturgical historians. First, an important series of articles by Marcel Metzger opened up a completely new line of approach to the text.[21] He developed an idea earlier advanced both by Jean Magne and by Alexandre Faivre,[22] that not only was it not the *Apostolic Tradition* of Hippolytus, it was not the work of any single author at all but rather a piece of 'living literature'. Metzger argued that its lack of unity or logical progression, its frequent incoherences, doublets, and contradictions all pointed away from the existence of a single editorial hand. Instead, it had all the characteristics of a composite work, a collection of community rules from quite disparate traditions. More recently, Christoph Markschies argued not only that the ascription of the *Canons of Hippolytus* to Hippolytus and the reference to him in the subheading of the *Epitome* were not made until the late fourth or early fifth century (and thus much too late to credit them with any historical reliability), but also that the apparent references to 'apostolic tradition' in the prologue and conclusion of the document had been

---

[21] Marcel Metzger, 'Nouvelles perspectives pour la prétendue *Tradition apostolique*', *Ecclesia Orans* 5 (1988), pp. 241–59; 'Enquêtes autour de la prétendue *Tradition apostolique*', *Ecclesia Orans* 9 (1992), pp. 7–36; 'A propos des règlements ecclésiastiques et de la prétendue *Tradition apostolique*', *Revue des sciences religieuses* 66 (1992), pp. 249–61.

[22] Jean Magne, *Tradition apostolique sur les charismes et Diataxeis des saints Apôtres* (Paris 1975), pp. 76–7; Alexandre Faivre, 'La documentation canonico-liturgique de l'Eglise ancienne', *Revue des sciences religieuses* 54 (1980), pp. 204–19, 273–97, here at p. 286.

misinterpreted by other scholars and consequently did not allude to the title of the work.[23]

In any case, the tendency to associate documents with apostolic figures or with those believed to have close connections to such persons so as to enhance their authority is very common in the ancient Christian world, and there are certainly other works that are known to have been falsely attributed to Hippolytus.[24] Yet even the very existence of a work entitled *Apostolic Tradition* by Hippolytus of Rome is not above suspicion. The list on the statue does not correlate exactly with the works of Hippolytus that are catalogued both by Eusebius and by Jerome. Very surprisingly, it omits those that are most strongly attested as genuinely his, including the commentary on Daniel,[25] and this has led some scholars to propose the existence of two authors or even a school of authors as responsible for the works on the list,[26] and Alistair Stewart-Sykes to build on this and argue that the *Apostolic Tradition* itself is the product of several hands from the same Roman school.[27] John Cerrato has gone further and suggested that because Hippolytus was a common name in the ancient world, the various works may be the creations of quite different and unrelated authors from diverse places.[28] In a final bizarre twist to the tale, modern research

[23] Christoph Markschies, 'Wer schrieb die sogenannte *Traditio Apostolica*? Neue Beobachtungen und Hypothesen zu einer kaum lösbaren Frage aus der altkirchen Literaturgeschichte', in Wolfram Kinzig, Christoph Markschies, and Markus Vinzent, *Tauffragen und Bekenntnis*, Arbeiten zur Kirchengeschichte 74 (de Gruyter, Berlin/New York 1999), pp. 8–43.

[24] See Nautin (ed.), *Homélies pascales I*, pp. 34–6; Jean Michel Hanssens, *La liturgie d'Hippolyte: Ses documents, son titulaire, ses origines et son charactère*, Orientalia Christiana Analecta 155 (Pontificium Institutum Orientalium Studiorum, Rome 1959; 2nd edn 1965), pp. 84–5; Allen Brent, *Hippolytus and the Roman Church in the Third Century: Communities in Tension before the Emergence of a Monarch-Bishop* (Brill, Leiden 1995), pp. 192–3.

[25] Hanssens, *La liturgie d'Hippolyte*, pp. 229–30, 247–9, 254–82; Brent, *Hippolytus and the Roman Church in the Third Century*, pp. 115–203.

[26] Pierre Nautin, *Hippolyte et Josipe. Contribution à l'histoire de la littérature chrétienne du IIIe siècle* (Éditions du Cerf, Paris 1947) and 'Notes sur le catalogue des oeuvres d'Hippolyte', *Recherches de science religieuse* 34 (1947), pp. 99–107; Vincenzo Loi, 'L'identità letteraria di Ippolito di Roma', in *Ricerche su Ippolito*, Studia Ephemeridis Augustinianum 13 (Institutum Patristicum Augustinianum, Rome 1977), pp. 67–88; M. Simonetti, 'A modo di conclusione: Una ipotesi di lavoro', in ibid., pp. 151–6; Brent, *Hippolytus and the Roman Church in the Third Century*, pp. 204–366; Paul Bouhot, 'L'auteur romain des *Philosophumena* et l'écrivain Hippolyte', *Ecclesia Orans* 13 (1996), pp. 137–64.

[27] Alistair Stewart-Sykes, *Hippolytus: On the Apostolic Tradition* (St Vladimir's Seminary Press, Crestwood, NY 2001).

[28] J. A. Cerrato, *Hippolytus Between East and West: The Commentaries and the Provenance of the Corpus* (Oxford University Press, Oxford 2002). See also his analysis of the current debate about the *Apostolic Tradition*, 'The Association of the Name Hippolytus with a Church Order, now known as *The Apostolic Tradition*', *St Vladimir's Theological Quarterly* 48 (2004), pp. 179–94.

has revealed that the statue itself was in origin not a representation of Hippolytus at all but of a female figure, which was restored in the sixteenth century as a male bishop because of the list of works inscribed on its base, using parts taken from other statues.[29]

If the new approach is correct, as my colleagues and I have argued that it is, then the so-called *Apostolic Tradition* is actually an aggregation of material from different sources, quite probably arising from different geographical regions and almost certainly from different historical periods, from perhaps as early as the middle of the second century to as late as the middle of the fourth. It is most improbable that it represents the actual practice of any single Christian community, but is best understood by attempting to discern the various individual elements and layers of which it is made up. Moreover, the composite character that the document displays extends also to the individual ritual units within the text, such as ordination, baptism, and even the eucharist itself, which appear to be artificial literary creations, made up of elements drawn from different local traditions rather than comprising a single authentic rite that was ever celebrated in that particular form anywhere in the world.[30]

Such a judgement obviously has very significant consequences for the status of the eucharistic prayer within it:

- It can no longer be taken for granted that it represents the form used at Rome or anywhere else as early as the beginning of the third century. Indeed, it appears to be a much later insertion into the developing church order and that the original eucharistic material in the text was the directions about a meal in chapters 25–27 – a view with which even the more conservative Alistair Stewart-Sykes concurs.[31]

- This does not necessarily mean, however, that the prayer was entirely a later composition. Some of the vocabulary found within it, especially reference to Jesus as God's 'child' rather than 'Son' and the use of 'angel of your will' as a Christological title (4.4), is distinctive of Christian

---

[29] See Margherita Guarducci, 'La statua di "Sant'Ippolito"', in *Ricerche su Ippolito*, Studia Ephemeridis Angustinianum 13 (Institutum Patristicum Augustinianum, Rome 1977), pp. 17–30; eadem, 'La "Statua di Sant'Ippolito" e la sua provenienza', in *Nuove ricerche su Ippolito*, Studia Ephemeridis Augustinianum 30 (Institutum Patristicum Augustinianum, Rome 1989), pp. 61–74; Hanssens, *La liturgie d'Hippolyte*, pp. 217–31; Brent, *Hippolytus and the Roman Church in the Third Century*, pp. 3–114; and Markus Vinzent, ' "Philobiblie" im frühen Christentum', *Das Altertum* 45 (1999), pp. 116–17, who made the intriguing proposal that the figure was originally of an Amazon woman named Hippolyta!

[30] See further Bradshaw, Johnson, and Phillips, *The Apostolic Tradition: A Commentary*, *passim*.

[31] Ibid., pp. 141–5; Stewart-Sykes, *Hippolytus*, pp. 31, 140–2.

authors in the first half of the second century and dropped out of use after that.

- On the other hand, other elements of the prayer, in particular the inclusion of the institution narrative (4.9–10) and also a quite developed form of epiclesis that asked God to send the Spirit on the oblation of the Church (4.12), have parallels only in literature from the middle of the fourth century onwards, and even then they are not found everywhere, suggesting that they were only just beginning to find their place in the rites.[32]
- At the same time, it lacks the Sanctus, which other prayers of that period seem to have already adopted (except perhaps for the Strasbourg Papyrus) – as a more integral part of their composition in the case of prayers of Egyptian origin and as a secondary insertion, to a more or less successful extent, in various Syrian texts.

This combination of older and newer features points to the conclusion that it probably attained its final form around the middle of the fourth century and that some version of the prayer was in existence from quite early times, even though it did not form part of the church order itself until much later, when it was updated with other elements that were then becoming current in eucharistic prayers of the period. Its earliest stratum appears to have been a substantial hymn of praise for redemption through Christ (a version of 4.4–8), to which a brief offering/thanksgiving formula (part of 4.11) and a short petition for the communicants were appended (the second half of 4.12) to make it suitable for eucharistic use.[33] There is, however, nothing that would connect this prayer specifically with any Jewish roots. Its style, structure, and vocabulary do not reveal any notable semiticisms. The only connection appears to be that, like its Jewish counterparts, it offers praise to God over food, although in this case not *for* food. Hence its initial composition seems to belong to a Gentile Christian milieu. Nor is there anything that connects the text specifically with Rome. Although there is nothing that can definitively exclude

---

[32] The institution narrative appears only in a rudimentary form in the *Sacramentary of Sarapion*, and seemingly was absent from the earliest version of the Anaphora of Addai and Mari, from the Strasbourg Papyrus, from the Jerusalem rite known to the author of the *Mystagogical Catecheses* and from that known to Theodore of Mopsuestia. The Strasbourg Papyrus also has no epiclesis and the *Sacramentary of Sarapion* an invocation of the Logos rather than of the Holy Spirit. See further Bradshaw, *Eucharistic Origins*, pp. 128–35.

[33] For a more detailed working out of this argument, see Paul F. Bradshaw, 'A Paschal Root to the Anaphora of the *Apostolic Tradition*? A Response to Enrico Mazza', *Studia Patristica* 35 (2001), pp. 257–65.

such a provenance, it is quite unlike what later emerges as the Roman eucharistic prayer, and because all its later accretions are similar to developments that were taking place in West Syria and to a lesser extent Alexandria in the fourth century, it appears highly probable that it acquired its later shape there rather than in the West.[34] Whether it is itself the source of these developments or simply one of several manifestations of them in eucharistic prayers known to us from the second half of the fourth century cannot be determined with any certainty.

Conclusion

While ultimately having their origin in Jewish meal prayers, Christian eucharistic prayers in a Gentile environment quickly left those roots behind, and apart from retaining the praise motif in the first part of the anaphora, reveal no overt connection to their parent. By the fourth century they had ceased to give thanks for food and drink and instead either offered praise exclusively for creation (as in the case of the Strasbourg Papyrus and the anaphora at Jerusalem known to the author of the *Mystagogical Catecheses*) or alternatively told the story of the saving acts of Christ at some length (as in the *Apostolic Tradition* and the Anaphora of St Basil) or combined the two (as in the case of the *Sacramentary of Sarapion*). Similarly, in their second half some prayed solely for the communicants (for instance, the *Apostolic Tradition*), others offered more general intercession (for instance, the Strasbourg Papyrus), while yet others once again, like the Anaphora of St Basil, combined both elements. The growing standardization of liturgical practices at this period ensured the spread of both the Sanctus and a narrative of institution to all known prayers by the end of the fourth century, as well as the inclusion of a developed invocation of the Holy Spirit in all those in the Christian East.

Perhaps not surprisingly, therefore, the quest for the earliest pattern of eucharistic praying reveals diversity more than commonalities, and the existence of prayers that for a considerable period of time were much less developed and explicit as to their eucharistic theology than were the beliefs of those who used them and preached about them. Thus they provide less than satisfactory models for modern liturgical compilers to imitate than do the more fully formed examples from later centuries.

---

[34] This argument is developed by Matthieu Smyth, 'L'anaphore de la prétendue "Tradition apostolique" et la prière eucharistique romaine', *Revue des sciences religieuses* 81 (2007), pp. 213–28.

Part 2
BAPTISM

4

Catechumens and the gospel

The conventional picture that has been painted of pre-baptismal instruction in the early Church is one in which catechumens attended public services of the word on weekdays and the celebration of the eucharist on Sundays together with all the faithful. At the latter they heard the scriptural readings and homily, and then were dismissed before the faithful began to pray together. While this picture may hold good for many places in the fourth century, a number of pieces of evidence lead us to question its universal applicability at that time and its reliability for any earlier period and to suggest a somewhat different scenario.

The *Didascalia Apostolorum*

When the heathen desire and promise to repent, saying 'We believe', we receive them into the congregation so that they may hear the word, but do not receive them into communion until they receive the seal and are fully initiated.[1]

At first sight this early third-century Syrian text looks odd, apparently expecting that converts would express their repentance and faith *before* they had been allowed to hear the word. Clearly, there must have been some preliminary instruction designed to bring them to repentance and faith. On the basis of the content of the 'Two Ways' material contained in the earlier church order from this region, the *Didache*, we might surmise that this prior instruction had been principally ethical in character. Nevertheless, it certainly appears that some specific teachings were reserved until after the candidates had made an expression of commitment to Christ, although it is impossible to tell from this short statement what those teachings might have been.

---

[1] *Didascalia Apostolorum* 2.39; ET from Sebastian Brock and Michael Vasey, *The Liturgical Portions of the Didascalia*, Grove Liturgical Study 29 (Grove Books, Nottingham 1982), p. 12.

The so-called *Apostolic Tradition* of Hippolytus

> And when those appointed to receive baptism are chosen, their life having
> been examined (if they lived virtuously while they were catechumens, and
> if they honored the widows, and if they visited those who are sick, and if
> they fulfilled every good work), and when those who brought them in
> testify in his [*sic*] behalf that he acted thus, then let them hear the gospel.[2]

As we have seen in earlier chapters,[3] this church order presents us with
some difficulties as to where and when the various elements within it
might have originated. This particular passage, however, seems to belong
to the oldest stratum of the document, and may well go back into the
second century.[4] It appears to envisage a similar situation to that in the
Didascalia Apostolorum: the baptismal candidates have already undergone a lengthy catechumenate, which involved considerable teaching,
but it is only now, after an examination of their conduct while they were
catechumens (rather than the profession of faith as in the *Didascalia*),
that they will be allowed to hear 'the Gospel' in the final stages of their
preparation for baptism. What was 'the Gospel'? Was it some particular,
secret text? Or Gospel readings in general? If the latter, then obviously
in this community, wherever and whatever it was, catechumens cannot
have attended a eucharistic ministry of the word of the type found in
later sources that regularly included a Gospel reading or they would
already have heard many Gospel passages. This conclusion receives some
support from the directions concerning the catechumenate that precede
the passage quoted above. They imply instead more informal gatherings
for instruction with 'teachers', who may be ordained or lay (15.1; 18.1; 19.1).
Finally, we may note that this appears to have been no isolated instance,
as Origen too was familiar with a separation of the catechumenate into
two stages with an examination of the candidates' manner of life (*Contra
Celsum* 3.51).

Fourth-century Syrian rites

Extant evidence from the fourth century in the region of Syria does not
indicate any exclusion of catechumens from hearing the liturgical Gospel

---

[2] *Apostolic Tradition* 20.1 (Sahidic version); ET from Bradshaw, Johnson, and Phillips, *The Apostolic
Tradition: A Commentary*, p. 104.
[3] See especially above, pp. 46–50.
[4] See Bradshaw, Johnson, and Phillips, *The Apostolic Tradition: A Commentary*, pp. 14–15, 108.

at the eucharistic liturgy. If that had once been the case, it had certainly now disappeared. The late-fourth-century *Apostolic Constitutions*, for example, locates the dismissal of catechumens after the reading of the Gospel and the homily.[5] On the other hand, John Chrysostom seems to have known at Antioch both a formula of renunciation of evil and an act of adherence to Christ that occurred on the day *before* the baptism itself. In one of his baptismal homilies delivered around AD 388, he says: 'Tomorrow, on Friday, at the ninth hour, you must have certain questions asked of you and you must present your contracts to the Master.'[6] Antoine Wenger advanced the suggestion that these rites had been moved back a day from the baptism itself in the late fourth century as a consequence of the large number of candidates presenting themselves for baptism,[7] and several other scholars have adopted his hypothesis.[8] But such an explanation does not seem very probable. Moreover, a similar pattern can be found in the rite of Constantinople in the fifth century;[9] and the testimony of Theodore of Mopsuestia and of the later Syrian rites also show traces of this same twofold structure, even though in these cases both parts now take place on the same occasion.[10]

It is tempting to suppose that the existence of an interval between the renunciation/act of adherence and the baptismal rite proper had some specific purpose behind it, and that, in the light of the evidence of the *Didascalia* and the *Apostolic Tradition*, the original reason was to allow time for the imparting of some particular teaching to the candidates. If so, we may presume that the interval might at one time have been greater than 24 hours, but that it gradually shrank when it ceased to have this function, until it is scarcely perceptible at all in the later rites. For what

---

[5] *Apostolic Constitutions* 8.6.

[6] *Baptismal Instructions* 11.19; ET from P. W. Harkins, *St John Chrysostom: Baptismal Instructions*, Ancient Christian Writers 31 (Newman Press, Westminster, MD 1963), p. 166 = *DBL*, p. 42.

[7] Antoine Wenger, *Jean Chrysostome, Huit catéchèses baptismales inédites*, Sources chrétiennes 50 (Éditions du Cerf, Paris 1957), pp. 79–80.

[8] See, for example, Harkins, *St John Chrysostom: Baptismal Instructions*, pp. 221–2, n. 37; Thomas M. Finn, *The Liturgy of Baptism in the Baptismal Instructions of John Chrysostom* (Catholic University of America Press, Washington, DC 1967), pp. 88–90.

[9] See Miguel Arranz, 'Les Sacrements de l'ancien Euchologe constantinopolitain', *Orientalia Christiana Periodica* 50 (1984), pp. 372–97, here at pp. 377–88; *DBL*, pp. 109–13.

[10] See Sebastian Brock, 'Studies in the Early History of the Syrian Orthodox Baptismal Liturgy', *Journal of Theological Studies* 23 (1972), pp. 16–64, here at pp. 22–3; Ruth A. Meyers, 'The Structure of the Syrian Baptismal Rite', in Paul F. Bradshaw (ed.), *Essays in Early Eastern Initiation*, Alcuin/GROW Liturgical Study 8 (Grove Books, Nottingham 1988), pp. 31–43, here at pp. 31, 34–8.

his evidence may be worth, the seventh-century West Syrian bishop and liturgical commentator James of Edessa claimed that after the candidates' renunciation and profession of faith 'the ancient custom was that they remained thus for a long time' before they were baptized.[11]

Apostolic Constitutions 7.39 describes a two-part catechetical programme: the catechumens first learn about the Old Testament history of salvation, and after that about Christ's incarnation, death, resurrection and ascension. A similar pattern is attested for Jerusalem by the late-fourth-century pilgrim Egeria, who states that during the Lenten season the bishop instructs those preparing for baptism for three hours each day, going through 'the whole Bible, beginning with Genesis'; then after five weeks he explains to them the meaning of the Creed, article by article.[12] Although no distinction appears to be made in either case between those allowed to hear the Old Testament and those allowed to listen to the doctrines of the Creed, it is possible that at an earlier time these had been two distinct stages, with the latter open only to those who had been accepted for baptism.[13]

Jerusalem was also familiar with an examination of the candidates' conduct of the kind found in the *Apostolic Tradition*, later known in the Latin West as a *scrutiny*.[14] Here it occurs at the very beginning of Lent when the candidates for baptism are enrolled. Egeria informs us: 'As they come in one by one, the bishop asks their neighbours questions about them: "Is this person leading a good life? Does he respect his parents? Is he a drunkard or a boaster?" He asks about all the serious human vices.'[15] Theodore of Mopsuestia describes a similar enquiry about the candidates' way of life that was put to their sponsors immediately after the registration of their names and prior to their exorcism.[16]

---

[11] See *DBL*, p. 62.

[12] Egeria, *Itinerarium* 46.2–3; ET from John Wilkinson, *Egeria's Travels* (SPCK, London 1971), p. 144. See also Maxwell E. Johnson, 'Reconciling Cyril and Egeria on the Catechetical Process in Fourth-Century Jerusalem', in Bradshaw (ed.), *Essays in Early Eastern Initiation*, pp. 18–30.

[13] On the two types of catechesis, see further Paul L. Gavrilyuk, *Histoire du catéchumémat dans l'église ancienne* (Éditions du Cerf, Paris 2007), esp. pp. 238–9.

[14] It should be noted that as time passed, the interpretation of this ceremony changed, from an examination of the candidates' conduct to testing whether the devil had been successfully driven out, linked to exorcism.

[15] Egeria, *Itinerarium* 45.3 (Wilkinson, *Egeria's Travels*, p. 144 = *DBL*, p. 33).

[16] Theodore of Mopsuestia, *Baptismal Homilies* 1.14–15; text and French translation in Raymond Tonneau and Robert Devreesse, *Les homélies catéchétiques de Théodore de Mopsueste*, Studi e Testi 145 (Biblioteca Apostolica Vaticana, Vatican City 1949), pp. 342–5. John Chrysostom refers to the candidates' sponsors (*Baptismal Instructions* 2.15) but does not explicitly mention a scrutiny.

Ambrose of Milan

What was it that we did on Saturday? We began with the Opening. The mysteries of the opening were performed when the bishop touched your ears and your nostrils. What does this mean? In the gospel, when the deaf and dumb man was brought to Our Lord Jesus Christ he touched the man's ears and his mouth: his ears, because the man was deaf; his mouth because he was dumb. And he said: *Effeta*, a Hebrew word which means 'be opened'. The reason why the bishop touched your ears was that they might be opened to the word and to the homily of the priest.[17]

It has been usual to explain this text by saying that Ambrose has here misinterpreted what was originally meant to be part of a pre-baptismal exorcistic ritual,[18] as evidenced in the *Apostolic Tradition*, where immediately after laying his hand on the candidates and exorcizing 'every foreign spirit that they flee from them and not return to them ever again', the bishop is said to 'blow' on them and 'seal their foreheads and their ears and nostrils' (by 'seal', is presumably meant 'make the sign of the cross on').[19] But such an explanation casts considerable doubt on Ambrose's intelligence. Could it really be that there was no tradition at all about the meaning of this particular ritual in Ambrose's community – that they just did it without any idea why – and that consequently Ambrose was forced to cast around to find some significance for it, and so proposed that it was intended as a parallel to Jesus' opening of the ears and mouth of the man who was deaf and dumb (Mark 7.32–7), even though 'sealing' would fit the immediate liturgical context better than 'opening', and even though it is the nose and not the mouth that is touched by the bishop? And if we suggest instead that it may not have been Ambrose who made this connection but some other Milanese bishop a generation or two before, then the hypothesis becomes even harder to sustain: could Christians there already have forgotten the meaning of the action at the beginning of the fourth century or earlier?

Let us then consider an alternative hypothesis, that there was a traditional meaning attached to this action in Milan, and that it did have something to do with 'opening', and so Ambrose's suggested parallel to the healing act of Jesus may not have been quite so wide of the mark after all. But such an opening of the ears only really makes sense if something aural is about to be delivered to the candidates. Ambrose tries to relate it

---

[17] Ambrose, *De sacramentis* 1.2 (*AIR*, pp. 100–1 = *DBL*, pp. 177–8).
[18] So, for example, *AIR*, pp. 17–18 and 100, n. 5.
[19] *Apostolic Tradition* 20.8 (Sahidic version); ET from Bradshaw, Johnson, and Phillips, *The Apostolic Tradition: A Commentary*, p. 106.

to the mystagogical catechesis that he delivers to the newly baptized daily during Easter week after their initiation. In the first of these addresses he tells them to 'Open your ears, then, and lay hold of the good odor of eternal life that was breathed upon you by the gift of the sacraments. This we signified to you when we celebrated the mystery of opening and said: "Ephphatha – that is, open up", so that each one who was advancing to grace would know what was being asked and would remember how to respond.'[20] This, however, seems to be stretching the meaning of the ceremony a little far, and it would make much more sense if some reading or teaching had followed immediately upon the liturgical action. Yet, just because there is no sign of the presence of any such thing in Ambrose's account is not to say that there was not once such a practice and that its remembrance was preserved in the retention of the accompanying ritual at that point. We may also note that, although catechumens were generally permitted to be present for all the liturgical readings and the homily at Milan, they were always dismissed prior to the ritual *traditio Symboli* or 'handing over of the Creed' to those of them who had been selected for initiation that year. This *traditio* took place one week before the baptism, following the scrutinies.[21]

As for the supposed existence of a parallel ritual elsewhere which was understood as related to exorcism, our only evidence for that is the *Apostolic Tradition* itself – there is no trace of it in any other early source – and while it is represented in the Sahidic and Arabic texts of that church order, it is absent from the Ethiopic text, which merely directs the bishop to breathe on the candidates after the exorcism (the Latin text has a lacuna here). Since it is not characteristic of the Ethiopic version to simplify the ritual details that it obtained from its source, we may suspect that it is the one closer to the earlier form of the church order and the 'sealing' in the others was a later development – perhaps even in imitation of the practice at Milan. I have to confess, however, that I am just as puzzled as Ambrose appears to have been as to why that ritual at Milan included the nostrils along with the ears:

> But why, you may ask, the nostrils? In the gospel, our Lord touched the man's mouth because he was dumb. He was unable to speak of the heavenly mysteries: so he received from Christ the power of speech. Again, in the gospel, the subject was a man; here, women are baptized. Nor is there the same purity in the servant as there is in the Lord, since the latter

---

[20] Ambrose, *De mysteriis* 1.3; ET from Boniface Ramsey, *Ambrose* (Routledge, London/ New York 1997), p. 146.

[21] Ambrose, *Epistula* 20.4; *Explanatio symboli* 1.

forgives sins, whereas the former has his sins forgiven, so that there is
no comparison between them. The bishop touches the nostrils and not
the mouth out of respect for what is done and for what is given. He
touches the nostrils so that you may receive the sweet fragrance of eternal
goodness . . .[22]

Rome

Then they are admonished by the deacon thus: 'Let the catechumens
retire. Let anyone who is a catechumen retire. Let all catechumens go
outside.'[23]

This directive from *Ordo Romanus* 11, which dates from the seventh
century according to its editor Michel Andrieu, belongs to the occasion
of the pre-baptismal scrutiny, which took place on three successive
Sundays in the Roman rite and was located prior to the reading of the
liturgical Gospel. Now it is clear from other evidence that at this time
at Rome catechumens were not regularly excluded from hearing the
Sunday Gospel readings. Is it possible, therefore, that their early dismissal
on these particular Lenten Sundays is a remnant of an older tradition when
they were not permitted to be present for any Gospel readings?

To this we may add the custom of the *Apertio aurium*, 'The opening
of the ears', in the Roman baptismal tradition. Although this ritual is
also described in *Ordo Romanus* 11 (nos. 44–60), it is in the Gelasian
Sacramentary that we first encounter the title, 'The Exposition of the
Gospels to the Elect at the Opening of the Ears'.[24] What followed was the
solemn reading of the opening verses of all four canonical Gospels to those
awaiting baptism at Easter, who by this period were of course infants and
not adults. The Gelasian Sacramentary does not make it clear exactly
when in Lent this ceremony took place, but *Ordo Romanus* 11 attaches it
to the third scrutiny, along with the delivery of the Creed and the Lord's
Prayer. Bernard Botte believed the custom to be a recent innovation,
developed when the genuine instruction of baptismal candidates in the
Scriptures had broken down as a result of the decline of adult initiands,
and entirely unrelated to the 'Opening' earlier spoken of by Ambrose.[25]

---

[22] Ambrose, *De sacramentis* 1.3 (*AIR*, p. 101 = *DBL*, p. 178).

[23] *Ordo Romanus* 11, no. 29, in Michel Andrieu (ed.), *Les Ordines Romani du Haut Moyen Âge*, II (Spicilegium sacrum Lovaniense, Louvain 1948), p. 425; ET from *DBL*, p. 246.

[24] *DBL*, p. 218.

[25] Bernard Botte, 'Apertio Aurium', in *Reallexikon für Antike und Christentum*, 1 (Hiersemann, Stuttgart 1950), pp. 487–9.

His case seems to be supported by the fact that the ritual of the *Effeta* continues to exist in the later Roman tradition as well, on a quite separate occasion to the *Apertio aurium*, on Holy Saturday itself, as it had in Ambrose's church.

On the other hand, Amalarius of Metz in the ninth century was familiar with a variant of this tradition in which the *Effeta* was performed instead on the day of the third and final pre-baptismal scrutiny, immediately before the reading of the opening verses of the four Gospels.[26] In another passage he affirms that it was 'our custom' for catechumens to be dismissed before the reading of the Gospel.[27] The Roman *Canones ad Gallos* of *c.*400 also mention an anointing that was performed at the third scrutiny, implying that it was the only occasion in the initiatory process when exorcized oil was used, but offering no explanation as to its precise meaning.[28]

This deficiency, however, is remedied by John the Deacon, writing at Rome at the end of the fifth century. He describes the scrutinies as involving a questioning of the candidates as to their beliefs followed by an anointing of their ears, nostrils, and breast: the ears, 'because through them faith enters the mind'; the nostrils, because 'they are thus without doubt admonished that for as long as they draw the breath of life through their nostrils they must abide in the service and commandment of God' and that 'they may be led unto his [Christ's] spiritual odour by the inner perception of a certain ineffable sweetness'; and the breast, because it is 'the seat and dwelling-place of the heart, so that they may understand that they promise with a firm mind and a pure heart eagerly to follow after the commandments of Christ'. Yet in the first two instances, John supplements these positive interpretations with apotropaic explanations: 'the ears being as it were fortified by a kind of wall of sanctification, may permit entrance to nothing harmful, nothing which might entice them back'; 'the nostrils, being fortified by this mystery, can give no admittance to the pleasures of this world, nor anything which might weaken their minds'.[29] It appears, therefore, that the action had by this time acquired a twofold significance.

Is it possible that what is preserved in Amalarius is a relic of the older practice, or at least *an* older practice, in which catechumens were not allowed to hear the Gospel read in church and so the ritual 'opening of the ears'

---

[26] Amalarius, *De ecclesiasticis officiis* 1.8.
[27] Ibid., 3.36.
[28] Canon 8 (*DBL*, p. 205).
[29] John the Deacon, *Epistula ad Senarium* 4–6 (*DBL*, pp. 209–10).

with exorcized oil preceded the revelation of the Gospels to adult baptismal candidates after the scrutiny had revealed their readiness for the completion of their initiation at Easter? John's twofold explanations would thus reflect both this older function of the ritual as well as its later reinterpretation as apotropaic. We may also observe that even the announcement of the forthcoming 'day of the scrutiny' (*scrutinii diem*) in the Gelasian Sacramentary describes it as being the occasion when 'the elect are instructed in divine things'.[30] The use of the singular, 'day', here rather than the plural seems to imply that originally the examination had been performed only once.

Something similar may at one time have also been the case at Milan, but it would seem that later developments were slightly different from one another in the two ecclesiastical centres. At Milan, as we have seen, the disappearance of the period of reserved teaching from its pre-baptismal location had by the time of Ambrose apparently led to the gap being closed and the Opening/*Effeta* ceremony deposited at the beginning of the baptismal rite itself on Holy Saturday, even though the delivery of the Creed remained one week earlier. At Rome, on the other hand, the ceremony seems to have remained at first at the conclusion of the third and final scrutiny, followed immediately by the symbolic reading of the Gospels and the delivery of the Creed and Lord's Prayer, and only later was it detached from there and moved to Holy Saturday morning, after the exorcism of the candidates and prior to the ceremonial *redditio Symboli* or repeating back of the Creed, though leaving its name 'Opening of the ears' behind with the symbolic Gospel readings.

Gaul and Spain

> *That catechumens are to hear the reading of the Gospel.* It was agreed that the Gospels shall be read to catechumens in all churches in our provinces.

This directive, canon 18 of the First Council of Orange (441),[31] strongly implies that previously the opposite custom had prevailed, at least in some churches in the region, and that catechumens had been regularly dismissed at the Sunday liturgy before the Gospel was read. A century later canon 1 of the Council of Valencia in Spain enacted similar legislation, demanding that the Gospel and homily should be heard by

---

[30] *DBL*, p. 215.
[31] J. D. Mansi, *Sacrorum conciliorum nova et amplissima collectio* (Florence 1759–98), 6, col. 439 (*DBL*, p. 256).

catechumens.[32] Pietro Borella judged the practices condemned by these synods to be merely recent deviations from the old established tradition of dismissal after the Gospel and homily.[33] But why should some churches have suddenly decided to change what is alleged to have been the universal Christian practice and forced catechumens to leave the church in the middle of the ministry of the word, especially at a time when the number of adult baptismal candidates was in decline? Is it not more likely that these churches were persisting in hanging on to an ancient local custom and that the councils were attempting to bring them into line with what was, now at least, the practice of the majority?

Conclusion

Individually these various pieces of evidence may not be thought to amount to much, but I would contend that cumulatively they build a case for the thesis that at least in some Christian communities in the second and third centuries there was a custom of reserving certain teachings to those in the final stages of preparation for baptism and not allowing them to be more widely known to the unbaptized, a custom that left traces in a number of places in the fourth century and even later. Using a comparative method not dissimilar from the one I have employed here, Maxwell Johnson has convincingly argued on the basis of evidence from a variety of geographical regions that three weeks had originally constituted the normal length of the period of final pre-baptismal preparation in many places.[34] One such piece of evidence is canon 1 of the Second Council of Braga (572), which mandates that 'as the ancient canons command' catechumens are to come for exorcism twenty days before baptism and during that period of twenty days they are to be taught the Creed.[35] Cyril of Jerusalem's pre-baptismal catecheses, delivered in the middle of the fourth century, are similarly concerned almost exclusively with the doctrines of the Creed and would have covered a three-week span.[36] This

---

[32] Ibid., 8, col. 620.

[33] Pietro Borella, 'La "missa" o "dimissio catechumenorum"', *Ephemerides Liturgicae* 53 (1939), pp. 60–110, here at pp. 60–72.

[34] Maxwell E. Johnson, 'From Three Days to Forty Days: Baptismal Preparation and the Origins of Lent', *Studia Liturgica* 20 (1990), pp. 185–201 = idem (ed.), *Living Water, Sealing Spirit: Readings on Christian Initiation* (The Liturgical Press, Collegeville 1995), pp. 118–36.

[35] *DBL*, p. 158.

[36] ET in Leo P. McCauley and Anthony A. Stephenson, *The Works of Saint Cyril of Jerusalem*, The Fathers of the Church 61, 64 (Catholic University of America Press, Washington, DC 1969–70). See also Johnson, 'Reconciling Cyril and Egeria on the Catechetical Process in Fourth-Century Jerusalem'.

seems to suggest that 'the word' (*Didascalia*) or 'the Gospel' (*Apostolic Tradition*) that had been reserved to the final period of baptismal preparation, which came after the confession of faith in some traditions and the scrutiny of the candidates in others, developed in most places into a three-week instruction on the articles of the Creed (as versions of that came into existence) solely for the ears of those about to receive baptism. This is supported by the fact that Cyril at the outset of his catecheses still urged his hearers to keep what they were to be taught during the period secret from other catechumens who were not yet enrolled for baptism:

> If after the class a catechumen asks you what the instructors have said, tell outsiders nothing. For it is a divine secret that we deliver to you, even the hope of the life to come. Keep the secret for the Rewarder. If someone says, 'What harm is done if I know about it too?', don't listen to him. So the sick man asks for wine, but, given to him at the wrong time, it only produces brain-fever, and two evils ensue: the effect on the sick man is disastrous, and the doctor is maligned. So with the catechumen, if he is told the Mysteries by one of the faithful: not understanding what he has been told, the catechumen raves, attacking the doctrine and ridiculing the statement, while the believer stands condemned as a traitor.
>
> You are now a man standing at a frontier: so, no careless talk, please. Not that these are not fit subjects for discussion, but that your interlocutor is not fit to hear them. You yourself were once a catechumen; I did not then describe to you the country which lay ahead. When you grasp by experience the sublimity of the doctrines, then you will understand that the catechumens are not worthy to hear them.[37]

The virtual disappearance of this phase of restricted pre-baptismal teaching from Jerusalem and elsewhere in the course of the fourth century, leaving only the vestiges we have catalogued, appears to have been brought about by the emergence of the season of Lent as a universal observance at this time. The period of final pre-baptismal preparation was thus extended from three weeks to forty days, and consequently there was a need to fill this longer span of time. The catechetical teaching that had previously preceded the three weeks would then have been drawn into it. We suggested earlier, on the basis of the contents of the *Didache*, that this preliminary instruction would have been primarily ethical, and it is interesting to note that the biblical readings prescribed for the Lenten catechetical assemblies in the fourth century tend not only to be drawn from the Old Testament rather than the New but also to give considerable emphasis to

---

[37] Cyril of Jerusalem, *Procatechesis* 12; ET from McCauley and Stephenson, *The Works of Saint Cyril of Jerusalem*, I, pp. 79–80.

those books from which moral lessons might be drawn. Thus, the Book of Genesis featured prominently in Lenten assemblies in both Jerusalem and Antioch.[38] And Ambrose in Milan, reminding the newly baptized of what he had taught them prior to their baptism, said: 'Every day, after the deeds of the patriarchs or the precepts of the Book of Proverbs were read, we preached a sermon on virtuous behavior so that you might be educated and instructed by these things ... Thus, having been renewed by baptism, you would hold fast to the style of life that befits those who have been washed clean.'[39] Furthermore, in the introduction to his *De Ioseph* he indicates the virtues that could be derived from the stories of the patriarchs: 'in him [Joseph] there shone forth above all the mark of chastity. In Abraham you have learned the undaunted devotion of faith, in Isaac the purity of a sincere heart, in Jacob the spirit's signal endurance of toils.'[40]

As this earlier teaching had been open to all catechumens, the distinction between the two stages of preparation was eventually broken down[41] and the rituals which had marked the transition from one stage to the next were either brought forwards, closer to the baptism itself, or put back to the beginning of Lent. Thus, at Rome the Opening/*Effeta* rite appears to have been moved, along with the delivery of the Creed, to the end of the original three-week period rather than its beginning, with the scrutiny now performed not just once but on all three Sundays, and then later the *Effeta* migrated still further to Holy Saturday itself. At Milan the *Effeta* rite seems to have moved directly to the Saturday in the fourth century, though leaving the delivery of the Creed behind one week earlier, as it also was at Rome. In the Antiochene and Constantinopolitan traditions the renunciation/act of adherence was first transferred to the Friday preceding the baptism and then much later into the baptismal rite itself, while in Jerusalem and in Mopsuestia it had already been combined with the baptismal rite before the end of the fourth century, although in both places the scrutiny had moved in the opposite direction, to the very beginning of the Lenten season.

---

[38] See Rolf Zerfass, *Die Schriftlesung im Kathedraloffizium Jerusalems*, Liturgiewissenschaftliche Quellen und Forschungen 48 (Aschendorff, Münster 1968), pp. 132–7.

[39] Ambrose, *De mysteriis* 1.1; ET from Ramsey, *Ambrose*, p. 146.

[40] ET from Michael P. McHugh, *Saint Ambrose: Seven Exegetical Works*, Fathers of the Church 65 (Catholic University of America Press, Washington, DC 1972), p. 189.

[41] A remnant of it appears to be detectable in Chrysostom's baptismal instructions, which he delivered at Antioch while he was still a presbyter, and in which he says that not he but 'the teacher', i.e., the bishop, will tell them about 'the faith' (*Baptismal Instructions* 11.18; ET in Harkins, *St John Chrysostom: Baptismal Instructions*, p. 166 = *DBL*, p. 42).

Furthermore, there was a desire to make the baptismal rite itself more secret and mysterious in the changed situation of the Constantinian era, when a genuine conversion experience could no longer be presupposed in those presenting themselves for baptism but needed to be induced through the drama of the rite. This seems to have resulted in most places in the retention of a period of reserved teaching, but transferred from before baptism to the week after baptism, when it could be used to reveal the hidden meaning of the initiatory and eucharistic rites for the first time to those who had just experienced them.[42]

The existence in early times of a period of pre-baptismal teaching hidden from other catechumens and revealed only to those about to undergo baptism does not require us to look to Gnosticism or pagan mystery religions for its origin: there are enough signs within the New Testament texts themselves of a tendency towards some form of secrecy within primitive Christian communities. Nor does it force us to postulate that the teaching consisted of certain mysterious 'secret Gospels', such as that alleged by Morton Smith to have existed but recently challenged as a forgery.[43] It could just be that Jesus' own words were considered too sacred for the Gospels to be read to any but the baptized and those who were about to be admitted into the fellowship of the faithful.

I realize that to some this suggestion may sound much too preposterous to be taken seriously. How could pagans possibly have been attracted to Christianity, and how could they have been converted to the faith and been willing to prepare for baptism, if the contents of the Gospels had never been fully revealed to them? In any case, early Christian writers themselves testify to the existence of knowledge about Jesus and his teaching among their pagan contemporaries.[44] But we must beware of reading back into Christian antiquity the presuppositions of our own age. We tend to assume that in order for a person to be drawn into a religious sect, it must be the central doctrines of that sect which attract them and win them over, causing them to change their lifestyle. In other words, we see

---

[42] Chrysostom and Theodore of Mopsuestia are partial exceptions to this rule, as both give an explanation of the initiatory rites in the period *before* baptism, and Chrysostom's post-baptismal teaching is primarily instruction in living the Christian life (*Baptismal Instructions* 3–8).

[43] Morton Smith, *The Secret Gospel* (Harper & Row, New York 1973). See Stephen C. Carlson, *The Gospel Hoax: Morton Smith's Invention of Secret Mark* (Baylor University Press, Waco 2005); Peter Jeffery, *The Secret Gospel of Mark Unveiled* (Yale University Press, New Haven 2007); but for a contrary view, see Scott Brown, *Mark's Other Gospel: Rethinking Morton Smith's Controversial Discovery* (Wilfrid Laurier University Press, Toronto 2005).

[44] See the examples cited in Alan Kreider, *Worship and Evangelism in Pre-Christendom*, Alcuin/GROW Joint Liturgical Study 32 (Grove Books, Nottingham 1995), p. 11.

the sequence as: believing first, belonging second, behaving third. But this is not necessarily always true, even for our own day, let alone for centuries and cultures long ago. In particular, the scrutiny of baptismal candidates described in some detail in the *Apostolic Tradition*, wherever and whenever that text might have originated, clearly focuses on testing the behaviour of the catechumens rather than their beliefs or the content of Christian doctrine, as a modern confirmation class would probably do instead. They were asked 'if they lived virtuously while they were catechumens, if they honored the widows, and if they visited those who are sick, and if they fulfilled every good work'.[45]

Thus, it rather looks as though it was behaving that was the prerequisite to belonging in the early Church, and that at least some believing might have been expected to come later. Indeed, it appears to have been the behaviour of Christians rather than their beliefs as such that was the principal attraction to the movement for pagans and the most effective means of evangelization. Christians would thus not have needed to tell them everything about the gospel in order to draw them into the catechumenate. The ethical precepts of the Lord might have been enough, and the deeper mysteries of the faith reserved for the time when they were ready to make the final commitment of baptism. This may have something important to say to us about how both evangelism and the catechumenate might be structured in our own day.

---

[45] *Apostolic Tradition* 20.1 (Sahidic version); see above, p. 56.

5

The profession of faith

Some sort of what we would describe as a profession of faith has been integral to Christian baptism since its inception, even in the case of infants, and I intend to argue that the evidence for the early forms of this act suggests a much more complex development than is often portrayed. In particular, I shall claim that the understanding of its nature changed quite significantly in the course of the first few centuries, and that it was this change that in part gave rise to questions and doubts about the propriety of administering baptism to infants which have continued to trouble many Christians down to the present day.

At the outset, however, it is important to take note of an important distinction that is often overlooked in the study of early baptismal practice, between formulae that might have been used catechetically and those that were used liturgically. The two are not the same thing, but in the past some scholars have presumed that if an author appeared to be quoting some sort of credal formula, then that must necessarily have been used in that form in the baptismal rite. Credal expansions of the attributes of God, Father, Son and Holy Spirit, do appear quite early in Christian literature. Justin Martyr, for example, in the middle of the second century speaks of the candidates being baptized 'in the name of Jesus Christ, who was crucified under Pontius Pilate, and in the name of the Holy Spirit, who predicted through the prophets everything concerning Jesus'.[1] But this apparent citation of a nascent credal formula does not mean that it was recited in that form within the baptismal rite. We would expect credal formulae like this to develop quite early in the Christian tradition – indeed, it has been claimed that some can be detected within the New Testament writings themselves – but the most probable use of these would have been in pre-baptismal catechesis. We should not make the assumption that they were being used liturgically without explicit testimony to that effect.

What appears to be the oldest extant instance of a form of profession of faith in connection with baptism is provided by the so-called Western

---

[1] Justin Martyr, *First Apology* 61.13 (*DBL*, p. 3).

text of the book of the Acts of the Apostles. Here in chapter 8, the account of the baptism of the Ethiopian eunuch by Philip, as a response to the eunuch's question, 'What is to prevent my being baptized?', this manuscript tradition inserts verse 37: 'And Philip said, "If you believe with all your heart, you may." And he replied, "I believe that Jesus Christ is the Son of God." ' We do not know whether this was the precise wording of an actual liturgical formula, nor, if it was, where it might have been in use, but it certainly implies that something like it was part of the living tradition of at least one Christian community through which a Greek manuscript of the Acts of the Apostles was transmitted and so was responsible for its textual elaboration at this point.

The *Didache*

When we look for further examples in early Christian literature in the East, it is rather surprising to discover that the *Didache*, which many would date as having been composed well before the end of the first century, contains no reference at all to a profession of faith among its instructions for the celebration of baptism. What it does contain, however, is an apparent indication of the use of a baptismal formula by the minister at the moment of immersion, seemingly in Trinitarian form, 'in the name of the Father and of the Son and of the Holy Spirit' (7.1–3), although some scholars have doubts whether these words are intended to refer to an actual liturgical formula as such,[2] while others believe the present text to be a later adaptation of an earlier version that used the name of Jesus alone.[3] It is even possible that the Trinitarian baptismal formula in Matthew 28.19 is also a somewhat later insertion into the Gospel.[4] If these claims are true, it would mean that baptism in the name of Jesus alone might well have continued into the middle of the second century, if not later still, in some parts of the ancient world. The criticism made by Cyprian of Carthage (*Epistulae* 74.5; 75.18) appears to indicate that the church at Rome in the third century was still willing to accept the sufficiency of baptisms in the name of Jesus alone, even if its own practice was now Trinitarian.

---

[2] See, for example, Maxwell E. Johnson, *The Rites of Christian Initiation: Their Evolution and Interpretation* (The Liturgical Press, Collegeville 1999, 2nd edn 2007), p. 46.

[3] See Arthur Vööbus, *Liturgical Traditions in the Didache* (ETSE, Stockholm 1968), pp. 35–9; Willy Rordorf, 'Baptism according to the Didache', in Jonathan A. Draper (ed.), *The Didache in Modern Research* (Brill, Leiden 1996), p. 217; but cf. Niederwimmer, *The Didache: A Commentary*, pp. 127–8, nn. 8, 11, and 12.

[4] See H. B. Green, 'Matthew 28:19, Eusebius, and the lex orandi', in Rowan Williams (ed.), *The Making of Orthodoxy* (Cambridge University Press, Cambridge/New York 1989), pp. 124–41.

Commentators have generally not remarked on the absence of any reference to a profession of faith in the *Didache* text, although J. N. D. Kelly did make the quite unwarranted assumption that an interrogatory creed was 'almost certainly presupposed'.[5] Nevertheless, it may be possible to shed some light on what seems to be a strange omission. The text mentions fasting beforehand, so why not a profession of faith? I have already argued in the previous chapter that, according to the evidence of the *Didascalia* and other sources, ethical instruction would have preceded the making of the profession of faith in the Syrian tradition and specifically doctrinal teaching would have been reserved until afterwards and given in the interval between then and the occasion of baptism itself.[6] We have no way of knowing how early this temporal separation of the baptismal profession from the rite as such came into being, but if it were quite ancient, it might help explain why there is no reference to a profession in the baptismal instructions in the *Didache*: it was not part of the immediate preliminaries of baptism but belonged to a prior stage in the process.

Fourth-century Syrian rites

Be that as it may, in the Syrian baptismal tradition the distinction between the two elements was maintained in later centuries, even though the interval between them became greatly reduced. Thus, as we saw in the preceding chapter from one of his addresses to baptismal candidates, delivered around the year 388, John Chrysostom seems to have known at Antioch a formula of renunciation of evil and an act of faith in Christ that occurred on the day before the baptism, which was now celebrated on Easter Eve.[7] In another such address, delivered two years later, he indicates that the words used by the candidate in what he describes as a 'contract' were: 'I renounce you, Satan, your pomp, your worship, and your works. And I pledge myself, Christ, to you.' And he goes on to explain that 'once you have made this covenant, this renunciation and contract, since you have confessed his sovereignty over you and pronounced the words by which you pledge yourself to Christ, you are now a soldier and have signed on for a spiritual contest'.[8] A similar pattern can also be found in the later rite of Constantinople.[9]

---

[5] J. N. D. Kelly, *Early Christian Creeds* (Longmans, Green, London 1950), p. 66.
[6] See pp. 55–6 above.
[7] See p. 57 above.
[8] *Baptismal Instructions* 2.20–2; ET from *AIR*, pp. 159–60 = *DBL*, p. 45.
[9] *DBL*, pp. 109–13.

That in the ancient Syrian tradition the profession of faith did not originally occur in close conjunction with the moment of immersion but some time before it suggests that its relation to baptism was viewed somewhat differently from those parts of the West where, as we shall see, the two actions took place concurrently. The profession of faith here appears as the moment of decision for the convert, and symbolizes a change of ownership and allegiance from the devil to Christ, especially in the more dramatic forms that it took in several fourth-century rites, when the candidate faced west to renounce the devil and then turned towards the east for the act of adherence to the person of Christ. It was the occasion of final commitment to Christ's service, which then admitted the believer to the inner circle of his disciples where he or she would learn the deep truths of the Christian faith that were hidden from unbelievers. Only after this teaching had been vouchsafed to the elect, would they go on to the final stage of baptism and incorporation into the number of the faithful. Thus, ritually speaking, the three stages of transition – pre-liminal, liminal, and post-liminal – are quite clearly differentiated here, and the profession of faith or act of adherence marks the movement from the pre-liminal to the liminal stage, and not from the liminal to the post-liminal.

Liturgical practice did not remain constant, however. Already we can see in the testimony of John Chrysostom's contemporary, Theodore of Mopsuestia, that the rite he knew had undergone further changes. Not only had the time gap between the profession of faith and immersion closed still further, so that both now took place within the one rite, but the act of adherence had become Trinitarian in focus rather than simply Christological: 'I pledge myself by vow, I believe, I am baptized in the name of the Father, of the Son and of the Holy Spirit.'[10] The *Mystagogical Catecheses* attributed to Cyril of Jerusalem tell of a similar modification in wording. The author states: 'Then you were told to say: "I believe in the Father, the Son and the Holy Spirit, and in one baptism of repentance."'[11] Later rites, while still retaining traces of the original two-part structure,[12] also reveal similar developments. Thus faith had

---

[10] Theodore of Mopsuestia, *Baptismal Homilies* 2.5 (*AIR*, p. 170 = *DBL*, p. 48).

[11] *Mystagogical Catecheses* 1.9 (*AIR*, pp. 74–5 = *DBL*, p. 31). For the debate about the authorship of the *Mystagogical Catecheses*, see the recent contributions by Alexis Doval, *Cyril of Jerusalem, Mystagogue: The Authorship of the Mystagogical Catecheses* (Catholic University of America Press, Washington, DC 2001), and Juliette Day, *The Baptismal Liturgy of Jerusalem* (Ashgate, Aldershot 2007), pp. 12–23.

[12] See Brock, 'Studies in the Early History of the Syrian Orthodox Baptismal Liturgy', pp. 22–3; Meyers, 'The Structure of the Syrian Baptismal Rite', pp. 31, 34–8.

ceased to be the gateway to an inner discipleship that would only later culminate in baptism; and in some cases what had been an act of personal commitment to the living Lord became an expression of belief in a more abstract Trinitarian godhead.

An even more significant change than this was also taking place at the same time, however: the attachment of the full text of a creed to the short act of faith. J. N. D. Kelly believed that this was what actually happened in the rite described in the *Mystagogical Catecheses*, but that the author abridged it in his description because he 'may have felt some compunction about setting [it] down'.[13] This seems highly improbable, because the pilgrim Egeria describes the candidates in Jerusalem repeating back to the bishop the Creed they had learned early in the morning a week before their baptism at Easter,[14] a practice that parallels that in some Western rites and almost certainly copied from there.[15] Be that as it may, we do find the Creed thus appended in the late-fourth-century *Apostolic Constitutions*, although the initial act of adherence is still directed towards Christ here and not the Trinity:

> And I associate myself to Christ; and I believe, and am baptized into one unbegotten [being], the only true God, the Almighty, the Father of Christ, the Creator and Maker of all [things], from whom are all [things]; and into the Lord Jesus Christ, his only-begotten Son, the first-born of the whole creation, who before all ages was begotten by the good pleasure of the Father, through whom all things were made, those in heaven and those on earth, visible and invisible; who in the last days descended from heaven, and took flesh, [and] was begotten of the holy virgin Mary, and lived holily according to the laws of his God and Father, and was crucified under Pontius Pilate, and died for us, and rose again from the dead the third day after his passion, and ascended into the heavens, and is seated at the right hand of the Father, and is to come again at the end of the world with glory to judge the living and the dead, [and] of whose kingdom there shall be no end. And I am baptized into the Holy Spirit, that is the Paraclete, who wrought in all the saints from the beginning [of the world], but was afterwards sent also to the apostles by the Father, according to the promise of our Saviour and Lord Jesus Christ, and after the apostles to all those that believe in the holy catholic and apostolic Church; [and I am baptized] into the resurrection of the flesh, and into the remission of

---

[13] Kelly, *Early Christian Creeds*, p. 33.

[14] Egeria, *Itinerarium* 46.5–6; ET in Wilkinson, *Egeria's Travels*, p. 145 = *DBL*, p. 34.

[15] See above, p. 60, and Augustine, *De symbolo* 11; *Sermo* 58.1. But note that in the West it was the handing over (*traditio*) of the Creed that took place on this day; the handing back (*redditio*) took place on the baptismal day itself a week later.

sins, and into the kingdom of the heavens, and into the life of the world to come.[16]

Although it may be objected that we have no way of knowing whether this text represents a liturgical rite in actual use or a fanciful compilation by the author, yet it is confirmed by other sources, including the later Constantinopolitan rite.[17] Some of them preserve the act of adherence to Christ alone along with the Creed, while others resemble Theodore of Mopsuestia's rite in substituting a reference to the Trinity instead. Indeed, it seems that even Chrysostom himself may have been familiar with the addition of the Creed to the act of adherence, in spite of his making no mention of it in his addresses to baptismal candidates. He touches on it in a sermon preached on 1 Corinthians 15.29 at Antioch a few years after those addresses. The absence of any reference to it in those earlier works could be because it was a subsequent development, but is more likely because the text of the Creed was still being kept secret, at least in theory, from those not yet baptized, as is evident from his obvious embarrassment in alluding to it in a sermon in front of both those who were baptized (and so would know all about it) and those who were not (and so should not learn about it):

> But first I wish to remind you who are initiated of the response which on that evening they who introduce you to the mysteries bid you make . . . And I desire indeed expressly to utter it, but I dare not on account of the uninitiated; for these add a difficulty to our exposition, compelling us either not to speak clearly or to declare unto them the ineffable mysteries. Nevertheless, as I may be able, I will speak as through a veil.
>
> As thus: after the enunciation of those mystical and fearful words, and the awful rules of the doctrines which have come down from heaven, this also we add at the end when we are about to baptize, bidding them say, 'I believe in the resurrection of the dead', and upon this faith we are baptized. For after we have confessed this together with the rest, then at last are we let down into the fountain of those sacred streams.[18]

It is not entirely clear at precisely what point in the initiatory process this took place. The reference to 'that evening', to being 'about to baptize',

---

[16] *Apostolic Constitutions* 7.3–8; ET from W. Jardine Grisbrooke (ed.), *The Liturgical Portions of the Apostolic Constitutions: A Text for Students*, Alcuin/GROW Liturgical Study 13–14 (Grove Books, Nottingham 1990), p. 67.

[17] *DBL*, p. 111.

[18] John Chrysostom, *Homiliae in epistulam 1 ad Corinthios* 40.2; ET from *NPNF*, First Series, 12:244–5.

and then at the end to going down into the water after the confession might seem to point to it happening during the baptismal rite itself at the Easter vigil and not in conjunction with the renunciation and act of adherence on the preceding day at the ninth hour. But, as Ruth Meyers has suggested, it is possible that the ninth hour could have been loosely understood as the evening, since services of the word at that hour often led directly into the evening office,[19] and the text does not explicitly say that the immersion followed the creed *immediately*. She goes on to conjecture that it actually took place on Thursday and not Friday, on the basis of a statement in Chrysostom's Thursday address that the candidates are going to say 'I believe',[20] but to presume that he must have meant on that very day and not on the next seems unwarranted. An alternative possibility is that liturgical changes had taken place in the years after his baptismal addresses, and the whole rite, including renunciation and act of adherence, was now celebrated on Easter Eve, as in the case of Theodore of Mopsuestia. On the other hand, when Theodore himself refers to the recitation of both the Creed and the Lord's Prayer, although he is not very precise, the context seems to imply that it took place on some unspecified day before the renunciation and act of adherence, in other words that it resembled the *redditio* that we find in the Jerusalem rite.[21]

The introduction of the recitation of a full creed into the rite is a perfectly understandable consequence of the moving of the profession of faith from before the period of credal instruction to its end. It would be natural for there to be a desire to sum up by this liturgical recitation what had been learned in the preceding weeks and in some cases to attach it to the solemn renunciation and act of adherence already present in the final preparatory rites. But the results were unfortunate, to say the least. The substantial text of the Creed greatly overshadowed the brief formula of adherence to Christ, sandwiched as it now was between a more lengthy renunciation and this doctrinal giant. Moreover, it had the effect of changing the implied character of baptismal faith, from an act of personal commitment to Christ to belief in a body of doctrines as the necessary prerequisite for baptism.

---

[19] Meyers, 'The Structure of the Syrian Baptismal Rite', pp. 39–40.
[20] *Baptismal Instructions* 11.15; ET in Harkins, *St John Chrysostom: Baptismal Instructions*, p. 165 = *DBL*, p. 42.
[21] Theodore of Mopsuestia, *Baptismal Homilies* 1.26–8; 2.1; text and French translation in Tonneau and Devreesse, *Les homélies catéchétiques*, pp. 362–9.

Early Roman practice

Before pursuing this important point further, however, let us first turn our attention to the practice of the profession of faith in the West, where, as I have suggested earlier, it appears to have taken a quite different form from that in the East. Unfortunately, when we attempt to ascertain what went on in Rome, our natural starting-point, we are faced with some difficulty. There is little evidence available for early baptismal practice here, and both of the sources which look as if they might offer us the best testimony are surrounded with problems of different kinds. Justin Martyr says that new Christians are washed 'in the name of God, the Father and Lord of all, and of our Saviour, Jesus Christ, and of the Holy Spirit'.[22] This description has commonly been understood as referring to a threefold interrogation and immersion of the candidate similar to that which we will encounter both in the so-called *Apostolic Tradition* of Hippolytus and in Tertullian in North Africa and which we certainly find in Roman sources several centuries later. But Justin does not explicitly say that this is what happens, and indeed he goes on to describe this 'name' as being 'invoked over the one who wishes to be regenerated'.[23] While it is just about conceivable that the Greek verb translated here as 'invoked' (ἐπονομάζεται) could mean that the baptizer questions the candidate about his or her belief in God, Father, Son, and Holy Spirit, its more natural sense would seem to be that the baptizer pronounces over the candidate the threefold name.[24] In other words, it appears that Justin may be outlining a baptismal practice of a Syrian kind, and not what later became the standard Roman way of doing things. This would not be all that surprising. Roman Christians were still at this period grouped in a multitude of local house churches, many of which doubtless had a strongly ethnic character, and as Justin was Syrian in origin and had been baptized at Ephesus, it is likely that he would have belonged to a community at Rome that was primarily Eastern in membership and hence in its liturgical practices.[25] If this is so, then the profession of faith may have taken place on an earlier occasion than the baptism itself. Justin may be referring to this occasion when he says that 'those who are convinced and believe what we say and teach is the truth,

---

[22] Justin Martyr, *First Apology* 61.3 (*DBL*, p. 3).

[23] Ibid., 61.10 (*DBL*, p. 3).

[24] Its cognate noun is used in the *Clementine Homilies* when speaking of baptism 'with the thrice-blessed invocation' (9.19, 23; 11.26).

[25] See *Acts of Justin* 3.3; 4.7–8, in H. Musurillo (ed.), *The Acts of the Christian Martyrs* (Clarendon Press, Oxford 1972), pp. 44–5. See also Andrew McGowan, *Ascetic Eucharists* (Clarendon Press, Oxford 1999), pp. 154–5.

and pledge themselves to be able to live accordingly, are taught in prayer and fasting to ask God to forgive their past sins',[26] as this certainly seems to imply an interval of some kind before the baptism itself takes place.

Problems of a different sort emerge with regard to the second source that has commonly been used to reconstruct pre-Nicene Roman liturgical practice – the so-called *Apostolic Tradition* of Hippolytus. As we have seen earlier, a growing number of scholars would now regard this work as a composite document, comprising several different strata added to the core at different points between the second and fourth centuries, and very probably stemming from different geographical regions.[27] This appears particularly true of its account of baptismal practice, and thus it can no longer be read confidently as a reliable description of what went on at Rome in the early third century. Nevertheless, in spite of this, when one strips away what seem to be later accretions from this part of the text, what emerges appears remarkably similar in a number of respects to what later became the standard Roman baptismal rite. These later accretions include extensive credal elaborations of the questions about faith that are put to the candidates. In the light of the distinction between catechetical and liturgical formulae that I made at the beginning of this chapter, it appears that these are catechetical formulae that have been artificially inserted into the text of the baptismal rite itself by later hands. They cannot be regarded as offering trustworthy testimony for actual liturgical practice without independent corroborative evidence, which in this case is lacking.[28]

As we saw in the preceding chapter, the core rite within this text appears to have known a moment of decision and admission to doctrinal instruction some time before the baptism itself. In contrast to the Syrian tradition represented by the third-century *Didascalia Apostolorum*, however, that door was opened not by an act of faith from the candidates but an examination of their moral conduct while living as catechumens. Here, therefore, the proof of true faith is looked for in the changed life of the candidate, while its verbal profession is deferred until the point of baptism, where there is as yet no indicative formula said by the minister. With the later accretions peeled away, the baptismal rite appears to have involved a brief threefold response by the candidate to questions put to him or her and accompanied by a threefold immersion in the water. Thus the candidate is asked, 'Do you believe in God the Father almighty?',

[26] Justin Martyr, *First Apology* 61.2 (*DBL*, p. 3).

[27] See above, pp. 46–50.

[28] See Maxwell E. Johnson, 'The Problem of Creedal Formulae in *Traditio Apostolica* 21:12–18', *Ecclesia Orans* 22 (2005), pp. 159–75.

responds 'I believe', and is immersed once. He or she is then asked, 'Do you believe in Christ Jesus, the Son of God?' and responds in the same way before being immersed a second time. Finally, the candidate is asked, 'Do you believe in the Holy Spirit?', and after answering is immersed for a third time.[29]

These interrogations at first sight seem to suggest that the primary focus of the rite was on the content of the candidates' beliefs rather than on their personal commitment to their Lord, as in ancient Syrian practice. But J. Albert Harrill has pointed out that the normal method of making a contract under Roman law, known as a *stipulatio* or *sponsio*, 'took a highly structured format in which one person, typically a prospective creditor, asks a question (*interrogatio*), and another person, typically a prospective debtor, gives an affirming answer (*responsio*) that must repeat the same verb as the question',[30] a particularly useful convention when the Latin language lacked a word for 'yes'. This cultural background implies that the original purpose of the baptismal questions and answers is therefore better seen as the establishing of a contract between the candidate and the triune God rather than as constituting subscription to specific articles of faith. Indeed, Tertullian in North Africa at the beginning of the third century described the process of repeating the words (*verba respondimus*) as being 'drafted into the army of the living God', likening it to taking the military oath (*sacramentum*) with which a soldier signed on (*Ad martyras* 3.1), thus anticipating by nearly two centuries the simile employed by John Chrysostom cited earlier.[31] Yet it strongly suggests that though the form of this interrogatory exchange may be different from the act of adherence found in the Syrian sources, its original purpose was apparently the same, the articulation of commitment, making a contract, effecting a change of ownership.

While the absence of any contemporary corroborative evidence means we cannot be sure that the core baptismal rite underlying the so-called

---

[29] Chapter 21.12–18, reconstructed; see Bradshaw, Johnson, and Phillips, *The Apostolic Tradition: A Commentary*, pp. 114–19, 124–7; Bradshaw, 'Redating the Apostolic Tradition: Some Preliminary Steps', in John Baldovin and Nathan Mitchell (eds), *Rule of Prayer, Rule of Faith: Essays in Honor of Aidan Kavanagh, O.S.B.* (The Liturgical Press, Collegeville 1996), pp. 3–17, esp. 10–14.

[30] J. Albert Harrill, 'The Influence of Roman Contract Law on Early Baptismal Formulae', *Studia Patristica* 35 (2001), pp. 275–82, here at p. 276.

[31] In fact, military terms were often used in connection with the catechumenate and baptism, especially by North African writers (see, for example, Tertullian, *De paenitentia* 6; Commodianus, *Instructions* 52–3), although it is an interesting choice of metaphor for a movement that was generally opposed to Christians enrolling for actual military service in the imperial army because of the nature of the religious oath soldiers were required to take and of the possibility that they would be called upon to shed blood.

Apostolic Tradition really does reflect early Roman baptismal practice, it is not dissimilar to two other sources deriving from neighbouring regions that are commonly thought to have closely paralleled what went on in Rome: Milan and North Africa.

Milan

Admittedly, Ambrose of Milan is a witness for the late fourth century rather than the late second-century date that I am postulating for the core rite of the *Apostolic Tradition*. Yet what he appears to cite as the formulae in use in his church do not differ much from what I have just described, and Ambrose was proud to claim that his local liturgical customs in general did not differ significantly from the practice of Rome. He says:

> You were asked: 'Do you believe in God the Father almighty?' You replied: 'I believe', and you were immersed: that is, buried. You were asked for a second time: 'Do you believe in our Lord Jesus Christ and in his cross?' You replied: 'I believe' and you were immersed: which means that you were buried with Christ. For one who is buried with Christ rises again with Christ. You were asked for a third time: 'Do you believe also in the Holy Spirit?' You replied: 'I believe', and you were immersed a third time, so that the threefold confession might absolve the manifold lapses of the past.[32]

Of course, one cannot rule out the possibility that Ambrose might have been here abbreviating what was actually said, but because he includes what appears to be an expansion of the formula, 'and in his cross', that seems less likely. Whether that expansion was actually in the spoken formula or is merely an interpretative gloss by Ambrose in his commentary is hard to decide. It is interesting to note that the Jerusalem rite too at this time seems to have acquired a similar threefold baptismal interrogation at the moment of immersion – another indication of Western influence there. The *Mystagogical Catecheses* state: 'Each person was asked if he believed in the name of the Father and of the Son and of the Holy Spirit. You made the confession that brings salvation, and submerged yourselves three times in the water and emerged . . .'[33]

North Africa

This second parallel source is more contemporary with the date I am assigning to the core rite of the *Apostolic Tradition*. From the allusions that

---

[32] Ambrose, *De sacramentis* 2.20 (*AIR*, p. 118 = *DBL*, p. 179).
[33] *Mystagogical Catecheses* 2.4 (*AIR*, pp. 77–8 = *DBL*, p. 32).

Tertullian makes to baptismal practice, it appears that he too was familiar with a threefold questioning of the candidates as to their faith in
conjunction with a threefold immersion. He states that 'when we have
entered the water, we make profession of the Christian faith in the words
of its rule',[34] and elsewhere that 'we are three times immersed, while we
answer interrogations rather more extensive than our Lord has prescribed
in the Gospel'.[35] What 'our Lord has prescribed in the Gospel' appears to
be baptism in the name of the Father, Son and Holy Spirit in Matthew
28.19, which Tertullian in his treatise on baptism describes as being
'a law of baptizing' and 'its form prescribed'.[36] How then are the interrogations 'rather more extensive'? Does he simply mean that a few more
words were used in each one, such as 'Do you believe in God *the Father
Almighty*?' Or does he mean they have been expanded in some other
way? Earlier in the treatise he had said that 'after pledging both of the
attestation of faith and the promise of salvation under "three witnesses",
there is added of necessity mention of the Church; inasmuch as wherever there are three (that is, the Father, Son and Holy Spirit), there is the
Church, which is a body of three'.[37] That seems to suggest that the third
question asked: 'Do you believe in the Holy Spirit and in the holy
Church?' Such an expansion also occurs in the baptismal questions in the
Testamentum Domini, one of the derivatives of the *Apostolic Tradition*,[38]
and half a century later than Tertullian in North Africa, Cyprian of Carthage
provides evidence for a similar expansion of the baptismal questions. He
asserts that 'the very interrogation which is put in baptism is a witness of
the truth. For when we say, "Do you believe in eternal life and remission
of sins through the holy church?" we mean that remission of sins is not
granted except in the church'.[39]

Later Roman practice

While it is not clear whether Cyprian is referring to an extension to
the third question, about the Holy Spirit, or whether he means that there
is an additional, fourth, question, the earliest official Roman liturgical

---

[34] Tertullian, *De spectaculis* 4 (*DBL*, p. 11).

[35] Tertullian, *De corona* 3 (*DBL*, p. 11). Tertullian also refers to a threefold immersion in *Adversus
Praxean* 26 (*DBL*, p. 11).

[36] Tertullian, *De baptismo* 13; ET from *DBL*, p. 10.

[37] Tertullian, *De baptismo* 6.

[38] See Bradshaw, Johnson, and Phillips, *The Apostolic Tradition: A Commentary*, p. 117.

[39] Cyprian, *Epistula* 70.2; ET from *DBL*, pp. 12–13; he attests to the same wording of the question when attacking the Novatianists in *Epistula* 69.7 (*DBL*, p. 12).

manuscript to provide the words used at the administration of baptism, the eighth-century Gelasian Sacramentary, apparently reflecting practice that goes back at least to the sixth century, manifests a similar credal expansion to the interrogatories in which the additions are appended to the third question:

> *And before you pour the water over him, you question him with the words of the Creed, and say:*
> Do you believe in God the Father Almighty? R. I believe.
> And do you believe in Jesus Christ his only Son our Lord, who was born and suffered? R. I believe.
> And do you believe in the Holy Spirit; the Holy Church, the remission of sins, the resurrection of the flesh? R. I believe.
> *And while you ask the questions, you dip him three separate times in the water.*[40]

Thus the original threefold questioning has effectively become sixfold – adding belief in the Church, remission of sins, and resurrection (or eternal life in the case of Cyprian). A fivefold articulation of faith, adding Church and either forgiveness of sins or resurrection to the Trinitarian core, is known in a number of other early sources, the oldest being the second-century *Epistula Apostolorum*,[41] and this eventually became part of the standard affirmation of faith in the later Coptic baptismal rite.[42] Because the earliest context for this formula is not explicitly baptismal, however, it seems likely that it first emerged as a catechetical tool and only later began to migrate into the baptismal rite itself. It thus provides yet another parallel to the Syrian tradition, where the original brief act of adherence gradually attracted to itself a complete creed. While this process seems to have begun much earlier in the West than in the East, the Romano-African tradition never developed the expansion to the same extent, because by the late fourth century there had emerged within the period of final preparation for baptism a separate solemn handing over of the full creed to the candidates and its repetition back by them. Thus by the time that the

---

[40] *DBL*, p. 242.

[41] Ch. 5, adding Church and forgiveness of sins to the Trinity; see Wilhelm Schneemelcher (ed.), *New Testament Apocrypha*, I (2nd edn, James Clarke, Cambridge 1991), p. 253. The expansion also occurs in the Latin version of the baptismal rite of the *Apostolic Tradition* (20.17), where Church and resurrection are added; see Bradshaw, Johnson, and Phillips, *The Apostolic Tradition: A Commentary*, p. 116.

[42] Adding resurrection and church (in that order) to the Trinity. See *DBL*, p. 135; Emmanuel Lanne, 'La confession de foi baptismale à Alexandrie et à Rome', in A. M. Triacca and A. Pistoia (eds), *La liturgie, expression de la foi* (C.L.V.-Edizioni liturgiche, Rome 1979), pp. 213–28.

candidates reached the baptismal rite itself, that element had already been covered, and so only the earlier short credal expansion remained attached to the profession of faith in that rite.

To sum up, therefore: the original purpose of the act of faith in early baptismal rites both Eastern and Western seems to have been to articulate the change of ownership and allegiance of the candidate, from the devil to Christ. While in the East this was expressed by the candidate making an indicative statement, the Romano-African tradition in the West employed instead the interrogatory form of making a contract that was customary in the surrounding culture, and gave this a Trinitarian shape from early times. Later developments added to this core further credal elements that had previously been employed in a catechetical rather than a liturgical context, more fully in the East than in the West, and in this way obscured its original intent and changed people's understanding of it. From being an articulation of personal commitment to a new Master, it came to be seen instead as a vocalization of the content of the candidate's beliefs.

Infant baptism

Yet, if we focus instead on its original role, it is possible that we may be able to make rather more sense of the emergence of the baptism of young children. As David Wright's studies have persuasively demonstrated, there is a lack of evidence to support the view that the practice of paedobaptism was universal in the early centuries, and in those places where it did take place, it often seems to have had more to do with the fear of the child dying unbaptized, because of the high level of infant mortality, than any fundamental conviction that all babies ought to be baptized.[43] On occasions when infants and young children were baptized, however, it seems that someone else made the responses on their behalf. The *Apostolic Tradition* gives the instruction: 'let their parents or another one belonging to their family speak for them'.[44] Tertullian also mentions the practice, although he is critical of it. He preferred baptism in general to be delayed, but especially in the case of little children, asking, 'For what need is there, if there really is no need, for even their sponsors to be

---

[43] See David F. Wright, 'The Origins of Infant Baptism – Child Believers' Baptism?', *Scottish Journal of Theology* 40 (1987), pp. 1–23; 'How Controversial Was the Development of Infant Baptism in the Early Church?', in James E. Bradley and Richard A. Muller (eds), *Church, Word, and Spirit: Historical and Theological Essays in Honor of Geoffrey W. Bromiley* (Eerdmans, Grand Rapids 1987), pp. 45–63; 'At What Ages were People Baptized in the Early Centuries?', *Studia Patristica* 30 (1997), pp. 389–94.

[44] Chapter 21.4 (Sahidic version).

brought into peril, seeing they may possibly themselves fail of their promises by death, or be deceived by the subsequent development of an evil disposition?'[45] A similar proxy action also appears to have been taken in the case of adult candidates who had signified their desire for baptism but were too ill to answer for themselves when the time came, although explicit evidence for this does not exist until the end of the fourth century.[46] The use of sponsors to answer the questions in the case of both babies and sick adults precisely parallels what happened in the making of contracts under Roman law. Because that procedure was entirely verbal, it was impossible for those who were mute or deaf or were infants to be able to make the *stipulatio* themselves, and so a slave or a guardian, known in Latin as a *sponsor*, might stand in for them.[47]

Thus what happened at Christian baptism was in line with the normal customs of the contemporary society. Just as parents and guardians were regarded as qualified to make important decisions on behalf of the children under their care in other aspects of their life, so too were they treated as capable of effecting the transfer of the child's allegiance from the devil to Christ. However, as that action attracted to itself more specific doctrinal content and the understanding of it consequently shifted away from the making of a contract to the articulation of a particular set of beliefs, questions began to arise in people's minds as to whether infants were competent to do this. At first different answers emerged. Thus, while Gregory Nazianzus in Cappadocia in 381 advised that children should normally be baptized at about the age of three years, when they were able to answer the baptismal questions themselves and could to some extent understand the Christian faith,[48] Augustine of Hippo put forward a justification for infant baptism that was destined to become the standard explanation in later Western theology: faith was not a prerequisite for baptism in their case as it was for adults, because faith was bestowed on the child through the faith of others in the celebration of the rite itself:

> when, on behalf of an infant as yet incapable of exercising faith, the answer is given that he believes, this answer means that he has faith because of the sacrament of faith . . . Therefore an infant, although he is not yet a believer in the sense of having that faith which includes the consenting will of those who exercise it, nevertheless becomes a believer through the sacrament of

---

[45] *De baptismo* 18.4; ET from *DBL*, p. 10.

[46] See Council of Hippo (North Africa, AD 393), canon 36; First Council of Orange (France, AD 441), canon 12; Cyril of Alexandria, *Commentarius in Ioannis Evangelium* 11.26; Fulgentius, *Epistula* 11.7; Gennadius of Marseilles, *De ecclesiasticis dogmatibus* 52.

[47] See Harrill, 'The Influence of Roman Contract Law on Early Baptismal Formulae', p. 277.

[48] Gregory Nazianzus, *De oratione* 40.28.

that faith. For as it is answered that he believes, so also he is called a believer, not because he assents to the truth by an act of his own judgment, but because he receives the sacrament of that truth.[49]

Incidentally, as this extract implies, and other places in Augustine's writings confirm, in his church the questions were now phrased in the third person ('Does he/she believe . . .') and answered in the same way ('He/she believes'), rather than being put directly to the uncomprehending infant.[50] This variation was enough to cause Augustine's theological opponent Pelagius to argue that, if adults and infants were supposed to be receiving the same baptism, then exactly the same words ought to be used in the rite.[51] Although there are signs that this form of the profession of faith was also adopted in Spain and France as well as Africa,[52] it did not apparently affect the liturgy at Rome, and so when the Roman rite eventually supplanted all other local rites in the West during the Middle Ages, the use of the adult formula for infants became universal, and effectively reduced the role of the godparent in the rite to that of a mere ventriloquist, supplying a voice for the silent child.

This practice has continued to raise questions for some as to whether babies can properly be said to believe. Yet if we return to what appears to have been the original understanding of the act – a transfer of personal allegiance rather than a statement of assent to doctrinal truths – that may set it in a different light. If parents and guardians (or even courts of law) are thought to be justified in making major decisions affecting the life of minors, then some at least would argue that they are also capable of doing so with regard to religious affiliation. However, it is quite a different question whether an obscure and obsolete method of making a contract in ancient Rome should continue to be used for this purpose rather than another form that would more clearly bring out what is really thought to be going on.

---

[49] Augustine, *Epistula* 98.9, 10; ET from *NPNF*, First Series, 1:410.
[50] See Augustine, *Epistula* 98.7; *Sermo* 294.12.
[51] See Augustine, *De gratia Christi et de peccato originali* 1.32.35; 2.1.1; 2.21.24.
[52] See J.-Ch. Didier, 'Une adaptation de la liturgie baptismale au baptême des enfants dans l'Église ancienne', *Mélanges de science religieuse* 22 (1965), pp. 79–90.

6

Varieties of anointing

One of the areas in which scholars have tried to fit together the extant evidence so as to create as far as possible a single, unified picture of a liturgical practice is that of baptismal anointing in early Christianity. Yet closer analysis suggests that this is far from having been the case. It is not just a question of whether it took place before or after the water bath or in both positions. As we shall see, there appears to be no consensus about any aspect of the matter, be it ritual form or interpretation.

The first three centuries

First, we need to acknowledge that among the earliest sources are some which make no explicit reference to any anointing at all in connection with baptism. Two of these in particular – the *Didache* and the description by Justin Martyr[1] – seem to exclude the possibility that anointing was actually practised but simply not mentioned, even though desperate attempts have been made by some to find hidden allusions to the practice in the respective texts.[2] In neither case does there seem to be any reason for the author to have omitted to mention such a significant part of the rite if indeed it had existed.

Second, our principal source for early Syrian practices, the *Acts of Thomas*, describes a variety of different forms of initiation rite. In the Syriac

---

[1] *Didache* 7; Justin Martyr, *First Apology* 61 (*DBL*, pp. 2–3).
[2] In the case of the *Didache* by reference to a prayer found only in the Coptic version of the text, which might, or might not, be about oil: see the review of the evidence in Niederwimmer, *The Didache: A Commentary*, pp. 165–7; to which should be added: A. H. B. Logan, 'Post-baptismal Chrismation in Syria: The Evidence of Ignatius, the *Didache* and the *Apostolic Constitutions*', *Journal of Theological Studies* 49 (1998), pp. 92–108; J. Ysebaert, 'The So-called Coptic Ointment Prayer of *Didache* 10,8 Once More', *Vigiliae Christianae* 56 (2002), pp. 1–10; and Huub van de Sandt, 'The Egyptian Background of the "Ointment" Prayer in the Eucharistic Rite of the *Didache* (10.8)', in Anthony Hilhorst and George H. van Kooten (eds), *The Wisdom of Egypt* (Brill, Leiden 2005), pp. 227–45. In the case of Justin Martyr, an older generation of scholars tried to read between the lines and discern allusions to confirmation there: see the works referred to in Bradshaw, *The Search for the Origins of Christian Worship*, p. 160, n. 65.

version of the text there are two instances that refer to an anointing of the head alone, associate this with the Messiah, and have no blessing prayer (chapters 25–27 and 132–33) and two that refer to the anointing of both the head and the whole body, focus on the theme of healing, and include a prayer for the blessing of the oil (chapters 121 and 156–58), as well as one (chapters 49–50) in which water alone is mentioned. In addition, in the Greek version of the text, there is no reference even to water in two cases: chapters 27–29 speak only of oil, and chapters 49–50 only of the 'seal' (σφραγίς, translated as *rushma*, 'sign', in the Syriac). While it has sometimes been argued that this word here refers to the rite as a whole, both anointing and immersion, its more usual import in the Syrian tradition is simply to denote anointing.[3]

Attempts have been made to harmonize at least some of these variant practices, most notably by Gabriele Winkler, who argued that the references to anointing of the head alone and those that included both head and body reflected two successive stages in the evolution of the ritual.[4] Ruth Meyers suggested alternatively that as explicit mention of the anointing of the body occurred only when female candidates were involved (who required the services of a woman to perform the action), in the other instances the body-anointing may have been presumed without necessitating detailed description, with the oil perhaps simply being allowed to run down from the head over the body or the apostle Thomas himself performing the service.[5] It is true that the only other extant reference to a distinction between head and body anointing from this period also occurs in the context of instructions as what to do in the case of female baptizands in the *Didascalia Apostolorum*, but it needs to be noted that here the anointing of the head is not specifically associated with the Messiah, as in the *Acts of Thomas*, but with the way that 'as of old priests and kings were anointed in Israel'.[6] Thus, the differences not only in what was done but how it was interpreted make it seem more likely that all these represent different parallel traditions that were known in the area rather than a single line of development. To complete the survey of the East, we should note that Origen was also familiar with a baptismal anointing of the body at Caesarea, to which he seems to attach an apotropaic function, as he likens

---

[3] See further Susan E. Myers, 'Initiation by Anointing in Early Syriac-Speaking Christianity', *Studia Liturgica* 31 (2001), pp. 150–70. For ET of all the relevant texts, see *DBL*, pp. 15–21.

[4] Gabriele Winkler, 'The Original Meaning of the Prebaptismal Anointing and its Implications', *Worship* 52 (1978), pp. 24–45 = Johnson (ed.), *Living Water, Sealing Spirit*, pp. 58–81.

[5] Meyers, 'The Structure of the Syrian Baptismal Rite', p. 41.

[6] *Didascalia* 16; ET from Brock and Vasey, *The Liturgical Portions of the Didascalia*, p. 22 = *DBL*, p. 14.

it to the smearing of the doorposts and lintels of the houses in Exodus 12.6–7, and so it too probably came before the immersion.[7]

In contrast to the Syrian witnesses, the earliest Western evidence for baptismal anointing refers to the action taking place after the immersion in water and not before. Tertullian in North Africa, writing around the beginning of the third century, describes an anointing of the head alone, which he compares to 'the ancient practice by which, ever since Aaron was anointed by Moses, there was a custom of anointing them for priesthood with oil out of a horn'.[8] In spite of the different position in the rite which this anointing occupies, the similarity in the justification given for it to that in the *Didascalia* might be thought to point to a common root reaching back to primitive times. On the other hand, it could just be that both were quarrying the same Scriptures to explain a practice the original meaning of which had been lost. Cyprian, writing in the same region half a century later, also mentions a post-baptismal anointing (without specifying whether it was the head or the whole body), but says that its purpose was so that the newly baptized person 'may be the anointed of God and have in him the grace of Christ',[9] while Hippolytus at the same period in his *Commentary on Daniel* (1.16.3) appears to associate the power of the Holy Spirit, 'with which, like perfume, believers are anointed after the bath', with oil,[10] in contrast to the North African writers who associate the Spirit with a laying on of hands.

The so-called *Apostolic Tradition of Hippolytus* introduces further complications to the picture of variant practices. Here there is both a pre-baptismal anointing by a presbyter with what is described as 'the oil of exorcism' following the candidate's renunciation of evil, and two post-baptismal anointings with 'the oil of thanksgiving', the first apparently of the whole body by a presbyter, the second of the head by the bishop. The first post-baptismal anointing is accompanied with the words, 'I anoint you with holy oil in the name of Jesus Christ', and the second with a Trinitarian formula, but no other specific interpretation of the meaning of either unction is given. In our commentary on this work, my colleagues and I argued that this is a composite text made up of different strata, and that the pre-baptismal unction and the first post-

---

[7] Origen, *Peri Pascha* 1.73–6.

[8] Tertullian, *De baptismo* 7 (*DBL*, p. 9).

[9] Cyprian, *Epistula* 70 (*DBL*, p. 13).

[10] Gustave Bardy and Maurice Lefèvre, *Hippolyte: Commentaire sur Daniel*, Sources chrétiennes 14 (Éditions du Cerf, Paris 1947), p. 100. On the disputed provenance of this work, see Cerrato, *Hippolytus between East and West*.

baptismal one both belong to a different, and probably later, layer than the specifically episcopal actions in this rite. At the same time we also raised the possibility that the anointing with oil by the bishop was itself a subsequent insertion into a post-baptismal sequence of episcopal actions that had formerly consisted simply of a prayer with imposition of hands, the making of the sign of the cross, and the exchange of a kiss – a sequence that may have some parallel in the rites known to Cyprian in North Africa.[11] If our reconstruction is correct, then all references to anointing may not have entered this text until around the beginning of the fourth century, as the oldest witness to it is the *Canons of Hippolytus*, thought to have been composed around 330. Even so, it would still be the earliest explicit testimony to a pre-baptismal anointing linked to exorcism, and to a full-body anointing in what seems to be in other ways a Western source.

What then can we make of this ante-Nicene evidence? The answer seems to be, 'not much'. Although nearly all our sources treat anointing as being a normal constituent element within the baptismal rite, they fail to show any agreement on either its position (before or after the immersion), its form (head or body or both), or above all its meaning – messianic/christic, priestly, grace/Spirit-filled, or what? This lack of consistency makes tracing its origin largely an impossibility. Moreover, when we move on to the somewhat more plentiful sources from the fourth century, the picture is still one with no greater agreement.

Pre-baptismal anointing in fourth-century Antioch

John Chrysostom seems to have known at Antioch in the late fourth century both a head- and a body-anointing before baptism. As we have seen in an earlier chapter, in one of his baptismal homilies (*c.*388) he refers to the renunciation and confession of faith taking place on Friday, the day before the baptism proper.[12] He states that an anointing of the forehead with the sign of the cross and a Trinitarian formula 'immediately' followed, and views this anointing as primarily being protective against the devil, although he also remarks that the chrism used is 'a mixture of olive oil and unguent; the unguent is for the bride, the oil is for the athlete'. He then goes on to mention very briefly an anointing of all the limbs, with which 'you will be secure and able to hold the serpent

---

[11] See Bradshaw, Johnson, and Phillips, *The Apostolic Tradition: A Commentary*, pp. 127–33.
[12] See above, p. 57.

in check; you will suffer no harm'.[13] Oddly, this appears to happen before the robe is removed for the immersion in water, and equally oddly there is no clear indication of the point in this sequence when the preliminary assembly ended and the baptismal rite itself began. However, in another baptismal homily (*c.*390), while he is not specific about when the preliminary rites occurred, he does make a clearer separation between the two anointings, stating that the second, specifically of the whole body, took place 'at the appointed hour of the night' and followed the removal of clothing. Here, in addition to the protective motif, he also states that 'the bishop anoints you as athletes of Christ before leading you into the spiritual arena', but this somewhat strangely in relation to the anointing of the forehead rather than more naturally that of the whole body, which again is dealt with rather briefly: this second unction is to 'armour all your limbs and make them invulnerable to any weapons the Enemy may hurl'.[14]

A similar double pre-baptismal anointing is described by Theodore of Mopsuestia, but in this instance both of them take place within the baptismal rite, and the first is interpreted primarily as receiving the identification mark of a sheep/soldier of Christ and the second as symbolizing the garment of immortality that will be received through baptism.[15] However, they are separated from one another by the ceremonial imposition of a linen cloth (called an *orarium*) on the candidate's forehead. As Ruth Meyers has remarked, it seems peculiar to place an *orarium* on the baptizand's head only to remove it immediately for the full-body anointing, and she suggests if the *orarium* had originally concluded a separate rite of renunciation, confession of faith, and first anointing, its position would no longer seem awkward (in later rites it is moved to a post-baptismal location to solve this problem).[16]

In the case of Chrysostom, and apparently of Theodore of Mopsuestia too, it seems that an earlier combined head and body anointing has become divided,[17] with the head anointing attracted backwards to form a dramatic conclusion to the preliminary rite of renunciation and profession of faith. This is suggested not only by Chrysostom's apparent

---

[13] *Baptismal Instructions* 11.19–27; ET from Harkins, *St John Chrysostom: Baptismal Instructions*, pp. 166–8.

[14] *Baptismal Instructions* 2.22–4; ET from *AIR*, pp. 160–1 = *DBL*, pp. 45–6.

[15] Theodore of Mopsuestia, *Baptismal Homilies* 2.17–20; 3.8 (*AIR*, pp. 177–9, 184–5 = *DBL*, pp. 48–9).

[16] Meyers, 'The Structure of the Syrian Baptismal Rite', p. 37.

[17] A suggestion made earlier by Finn, *The Liturgy of Baptism in the Baptismal Instructions of St John Chrysostom*, p. 119.

vagueness with regard to where one ended and the other began but also by his explanation of the meaning of the first anointing, which would make more natural sense if it were in relation to a whole head and body unction rather than of the forehead alone, and which leaves him with nothing much to say about the second anointing, of the whole body. It is also supported by evidence from other rites that are thought to derive from that of Antioch, where the head and body anointings are still united in the baptismal rite itself. Thus, the fifth-century rite of Constantinople, where the renunciation and confession of faith continued to constitute a separate rite on Good Friday, as had been the case in Chrysostom's Antioch, has no anointing of the head there, but instead a simple imposition of the hand and blessing by the patriarch concludes it.[18] Pseudo-Dionysius also describes the profession of faith as being followed by an imposition of hands, with the anointing of the head and body both taking place after the candidate has been unclothed: the bishop 'begins the anointing with the threefold sealing, and for the rest assigns the man to the priests for the anointing of his whole body', while he begins the consecration of the baptismal water.[19] It appears, therefore, that Chrysostom's experimental repositioning of the anointing of the head was not one that lasted.

Pre-baptismal anointing in later Syrian practice

In support of the above contention, it is to be noted that some later Syrian liturgical texts continue to mark an earlier division between the preliminary rites, which include the renunciation and profession of faith, and the baptismal rite proper, and in every instance locate all anointings in the second part. However, nearly all the extant texts speak of two separate pre-baptismal anointings, one coming before the consecration of the water and the other after.[20] Although there is some variation, the first anointing is usually of the forehead alone, while the second involves the anointing of the head by the priest and of the rest of the body by deacons. In the earliest manuscripts of the rite, the formula accompanying the first of these speaks of the 'oil of gladness'[21] which will make the candidate 'worthy

---

[18] *DBL*, pp. 109–13.

[19] Pseudo-Dionysius, *De ecclesiastica hierarchia* 2.2.6–7 (*DBL*, p. 61).

[20] See Brock, 'Studies in the Early History of the Syrian Orthodox Baptismal Liturgy', pp. 23–4.

[21] This expression, found in Isaiah 61.3, Psalm 45.7, and Hebrews 1.9, is also used of the baptismal oil both by *Apostolic Constitutions* 2.32.3 and by Chrysostom but without any clear indication that it was employed in a liturgical formula as such: see Harkins, *St John Chrysostom: Baptismal Instructions*, p. 58.

of the adoption of rebirth', while a preceding prayer asks for the gift of the Holy Spirit. The formula accompanying the second refers both to protection against the devil and to grafting into the good olive tree of the Church, an apparent allusion to Romans 11.[22]

Sebastian Brock has suggested that, as in the case of Chrysostom, this double unction is also the result of the duplication of a single anointing, which came about because, he alleges, its original position varied, in some cases preceding the consecration of the water, in others following it, and because it was already a twofold action, the priest anointing the head, the deacons the rest of the body.[23] This explanation, however, fails to take seriously the fact that the anointing of the head is repeated in the second unction (Brock simply remarks that the anointing of the body 'was unlikely to be kept alone') and the fact that Pseudo-Dionysius and other Syrian commentators refer only to a single anointing, before the consecration of the water, as well as the fact that the Byzantine and East Syrian rites too only know of a single pre-baptismal anointing.[24] Brock does point out, however, that the theme of grafting in Romans 11 is quite unknown in connection with baptism in any Antiochene writer of the first five centuries, but because it is found in the Jerusalem *Mystagogical Catecheses* in connection with the pre-baptismal anointing, he postulates that 'when the post-baptismal anointing was introduced from Jerusalem into the Antiochene rite, there came with it the Jerusalem formula for the pre-baptismal anointing as well'.[25]

This suggestion may, however, be taken further. Could it have been that not just the formula but the whole head and body anointing itself was imported from Jerusalem into the Syrian rite at the same time as the post-baptismal unction, and placed immediately before the immersion, as it had been at Jerusalem? If this hypothesis is correct, it would mean that previously the rite into which it was inserted had only had one anointing, of the head alone, which took place before the consecration of the water. Yet this contrasts both with the custom known to Chrysostom and with the single head and body anointing recorded in Pseudo-Dionysius and also found in East Syrian and Byzantine practice. On the other hand, it is in continuity with what we have proposed was the earlier varied tradition of this region, where some communities knew

---

[22] Brock, 'Studies in the Early History of the Syrian Orthodox Baptismal Liturgy', pp. 29–30, 32.

[23] Ibid., pp. 36–7.

[24] See *DBL*, pp. 61, 68–9, 122.

[25] Brock, 'Studies in the Early History of the Syrian Orthodox Baptismal Liturgy', p. 39.

an anointing of the head and body associated with healing while others had just an anointing of the head alone associated with the Messiah. It is to be noted that the prayer preceding the anointing of the head in these Syrian liturgical texts continues to make reference to the gift of the Spirit. Furthermore, there are a small number of Syrian sources that do make mention of a pre-baptismal anointing of the head alone, which may be remnants of this earlier tradition. Brock mentions several liturgical texts, including one tenth-century manuscript in particular (BM Add. 14493, ff. 165–70), where an anointing of the head alone occurs, although the accompanying formula has obviously been influenced by rites where there was also an anointing of the head and body.[26] He also published a translation of a Syrian baptismal commentary, the oldest recension of which mentions only a pre-baptismal anointing of the head and which he dated to the early fifth century.[27] Brock believes that these all reflect the older practice stemming from Tagrit over against the Antiochene tradition recorded in Chrysostom.

The testimony of the fourth-century Syrian *Apostolic Constitutions* with regard to pre-baptismal anointing is somewhat ambiguous. Book 7 speaks only of one such anointing, which apparently follows the confession of faith and precedes the consecration of the water, and is associated with the Holy Spirit (7.42; see also 7.22). It might be thought that this unction was applied to the head alone but the text does not make that clear. On the other hand, in Book 3 the baptismal instructions of the third-century *Didascalia* with its head and body anointing have been preserved and reworked in a somewhat confusing manner which seems to speak of two anointings of the head, one by a deacon and the other by the bishop, as well as the anointing of the body.[28]

Nevertheless, taken as a whole, the evidence from this region suggests that the early variety of practice to which the ante-Nicene sources point continued to have an influence in later centuries. On the one hand, Chrysostom and Pseudo-Dionysius in particular bear witness to the persistence in Antioch for some time of a head and body anointing that was understood primarily as protective against the power of evil. On the other hand, later Syrian sources appear to indicate the existence elsewhere in the region of an original anointing of the head alone linked to the Holy

---

[26] Ibid., pp. 21, 30 (especially n. 2), and 39.
[27] Sebastian Brock, 'Some Early Syrian Baptismal Commentaries', *Orientalia Christiana Periodica* 46 (1980), pp. 20–61.
[28] *DBL*, pp. 36–8.

Spirit, which only later under the influence of Jerusalem had been supplemented with a head and body anointing that referred to the themes of grafting-in and protection. The association of the Holy Spirit with the baptismal water that is made in Chrysostom's rite is usually said to be the result of a transfer from an earlier association with the pre-baptismal anointing. Yet if that rite traces its parentage back to a tradition of whole-body anointing that was concerned with healing rather than to a head anointing which was associated with the Messiah or his Spirit, it may not be so much a matter of development as of continuing fidelity to that particular older understanding.

Jerusalem

According to the author of the *Mystagogical Catecheses* (whether Cyril or someone else), the practice in Jerusalem was for exorcized oil to be applied to the candidates' whole body immediately prior to their going into the water, which he interprets as making them 'sharers in Jesus Christ, who is the cultivated olive tree. For you have been separated from the wild olive tree and grafted on to the cultivated olive tree, and given a share in the richness of the true olive.' The exorcized oil also 'drives away every trace of the enemy's power' and is able 'to pursue all the invisible powers of the wicked one out of our persons'.[29] A post-baptismal unction of the forehead, ears, nostrils, and chest by which the Holy Spirit was imparted is also described, and an explanation given for the choice of the parts of the body involved: the forehead, 'so that you might lose the shame which Adam, the first transgressor everywhere bore with him, and so that you might "with unveiled face behold the glory of the Lord"'; the ears, 'that you might acquire ears which will hear those divine mysteries of which Isaiah said: "The Lord has given me an ear to hear with"'; the nostrils, 'so that after receiving the divine chrism you might say: "We are the aroma of Christ to God among those who are being saved"'; and the chest, 'so that "having put on the breast-plate of righteousness, you might stand against the wiles of the devil"'.[30] As Juliette Day has observed, none of these explanations is explicitly Christological or pneumatological.[31] This suggests the possibility that their combination with the bestowal of the Spirit may be a secondary development.

---

[29] *Mystagogical Catecheses* 2.3 (*AIR*, p. 77).
[30] Ibid., 3.4 (*AIR*, pp. 83–4).
[31] Day, *The Baptismal Liturgy of Jerusalem*, p. 111.

While both these anointings, before and after baptism, were subsequently copied in Syria and beyond, as indicated above, they differ markedly from what we know of contemporary practice in the region. Other Syrian rites of the time do not view the pre-baptismal unction as primarily exorcistic, nor do they employ exorcized oil for the purpose. Neither Chrysostom nor the East Syrian rites are familiar with a post-baptismal anointing at all, and while Theodore of Mopsuestia does apparently speak of a post-baptismal 'sealing' that seems to have included the use of oil and was related to the gift of the Holy Spirit, this was of the forehead alone.[32] Similarly, there are references in the *Apostolic Constitutions* to a post-baptismal anointing with chrism by the bishop, but it too is simply described as a 'seal' (the Holy Spirit here still being associated with the pre-baptismal unction) and there is no hint of it being applied to the organs of sense.[33]

Whence, then, might the Jerusalem practices have been derived? Both Geoffrey Cuming and Bryan Spinks many years ago suggested the possibility of Egyptian influence on the Jerusalem initiation rites,[34] and recently Juliette Day has cautiously supported the idea that the source of the Jerusalem pre-baptismal anointing in particular may have been Egypt, although she is somewhat more sceptical about the post-baptismal unction being derived from there as well.[35] Therefore it is to Egypt that we now turn.

Egypt

The fourth-century *Canons of Hippolytus* retains a pre-baptismal anointing with the oil of exorcism immediately after the renunciation and before the confession of faith, as was the case in the so-called *Apostolic Tradition of Hippolytus*. Whether this is simply fidelity to its principal source or reflects actual practice in Egypt cannot be determined, although in the later Coptic rite there is an anointing of the chest, arms, heart, and hands immediately after the renunciation and profession of faith.[36] However, in the *Canons of Hippolytus* some changes are made to the post-baptismal

---

[32] Theodore of Mopsuestia, *Baptismal Homilies* 3.27 (*AIR*, pp. 198–9; see also ibid., n. 65, for discussion of those questioning the authenticity of the reference to oil here).

[33] *Apostolic Constitutions* 3.16–17; 7.22, 44 (*DBL*, pp. 36–9).

[34] Geoffrey J. Cuming, 'Egyptian Elements in the Jerusalem Liturgy', *Journal of Theological Studies* 25 (1974), pp. 117–24, here at p. 123; Bryan D. Spinks, 'The Jerusalem Liturgy of the *Catecheses Mystagogicae*: Syrian or Egyptian?', *Studia Patristica* 18 (1989), pp. 391–5.

[35] Day, *The Baptismal Liturgy of Jerusalem*, pp. 74–7, 116–19.

[36] See *DBL*, p. 136.

prescriptions of the *Apostolic Tradition*, which therefore do seem to point to what was actually done in the place from which this text originated, even though a post-baptismal unction may not yet have been part of the practice of the patriarchal see at Alexandria. The presbyter is directed to sign the forehead, mouth, and chest of the newly baptized, in addition to anointing all the body, head, and face, while using a Trinitarian formula rather than the Christic one in the *Apostolic Tradition*. The second post-baptismal anointing from that source is reduced to a simple signing of the forehead with oil (and in one manuscript even this reference is replaced with 'the sign of charity') without any formula being specified.[37] The mid-fourth-century *Sacramentary of Sarapion* also contains two prayers for use over oils for what are clearly intended for pre- and post-baptismal unction, the former emphasizing healing and protection and the latter (over chrism) the gift of the Holy Spirit and the power of the sealing.[38]

One unique fourth-century parallel between the *Canons of Hippolytus* and the Jerusalem rite is the use of exorcized oil for the pre-baptismal anointing. The two also share in common a post-baptismal unction in which various parts of the body are anointed – but not precisely the same parts, and in the *Canons* it is not explicitly associated with the Holy Spirit. These resemblances alone are insufficient to demonstrate a direct relationship, but they do imply that both have emerged from a similar world or have been influenced by a common source. Juliette Day speculates that the link might have been some version of the *Apostolic Tradition* that was circulating in Egypt and West Syria, and that might also have been responsible for the introduction of the post-baptismal anointing in the *Apostolic Constitutions*.[39] However, as will be pointed out in our conclusions, the truth seems likely to have been rather more complicated than that.

The West

References to baptismal anointing in the West are very sparse during the fourth century. The only place where a pre-baptismal anointing is clearly attested is at Milan. In his treatise *De sacramentis* Ambrose describes it as taking place immediately after the entry into the baptistery and prior to the renunciation – a different position from any we have encountered so far. It was apparently of the whole body, performed by a deacon and a

---

[37] Ibid., pp. 130–2.
[38] Prayers 15, 16 (*DBL*, pp. 126–7).
[39] Day, *The Baptismal Liturgy of Jerusalem*, pp. 119, 138.

presbyter, and Ambrose likens it to an athlete being prepared for a wrestling match.[40] It does not appear to have been thought particularly significant theologically as it is given only brief and superficial treatment here by Ambrose and not mentioned at all in his *De mysteriis*. Could it have been a recent import in imitation of practice elsewhere? After the immersion, Ambrose describes an anointing with chrism by the bishop 'to eternal life', performed over the head because 'the faculties of the wise man are situated in his head'.[41] This is followed by the washing of the feet of the newly baptized and then something called 'the spiritual seal' connected to the sevenfold gifts of the Holy Spirit, but it is not at all clear what ritual action was involved in this besides prayer by the bishop.[42] For Rome, we have to wait until the end of the century to encounter firm evidence for the practice of anointing with exorcized oil in preparation for baptism, although nothing is said about its use in the baptismal rite proper,[43] and to 416 for our first reference (outside the *Apostolic Tradition* and its derivatives) to a double post-baptismal anointing, the first being performed by presbyters and the second by the bishop, and this latter being understood as conveying the Holy Spirit.[44]

Conclusion

The variety that we asserted characterized the roots of baptismal anointing in the Christian tradition clearly persists in the fourth century onward. Both the anointing of the head and the anointing of the whole body before baptism continue to be visible in the developing Eastern rites, even though explanations for them gradually change. Pre-baptismal anointing seems to have been slower to emerge in the West, and the use for that purpose of exorcized oil both at Rome and in Jerusalem does encourage the thought that the influence of the *Apostolic Tradition*, or of the source behind that part of its initiation material, may have contributed to that particular development as well as to the ultimate appearance of a second post-baptismal anointing in the Roman tradition. With regard to post-baptismal anointing, it is not simply a matter of migration

---

[40] Ambrose, *De sacramentis* 1.4 (*AIR*, pp. 101–2 = *DBL*, p. 178).

[41] This quotation is adapted by Ambrose from Ecclesiastes 2.14.

[42] Ambrose, *De sacramentis* 2.24; 3.1–10 (*AIR*, pp. 119–25). This account is paralleled in *De mysteriis* 6.29–30, 41–2. For discussion of the nature of the spiritual seal, see Pamela Jackson, 'The Meaning of "Spirituale Signaculum" in the Mystagogy of Ambrose of Milan', *Ecclesia Orans* 7 (1990), pp. 77–94; Johnson, *The Rites of Christian Initiation*, pp. 171–5.

[43] *Canones ad Gallos*, canon 8 (*DBL*, p. 205).

[44] Letter of Innocent I to Decentius (*DBL*, p. 206).

from West to East as pre-baptismal anointing may have been exported from East to West, though that may well be part of the story. The appearance in both Egypt and Jerusalem of anointing of parts of the body – but not the same parts, and neither of them including the eyes and mouth as in later Eastern traditions – suggests influence from elsewhere. Although Alistair Logan's attempts to find early evidence for the existence of a post-baptismal anointing in Syria will for the most part not stand up to close scrutiny, his claim that there existed a Gnostic initiation ritual involving both water and the anointing of the five senses seems to have more merit,[45] and the practice may have percolated from there into more mainstream Christian usage.[46] In short, there appear to have been at least three main distinct strands in the emergence of post-baptismal anointing in the East: (1) the addition in some places of a post-baptismal unction, generally of the head, not directly related to the gift of the Spirit but commonly understood as 'sealing' in some way; (2) the addition in others of an alternative form of such anointing, involving the senses and/or other parts of the body, possibly derived from Christian Gnostic circles; and (3) the subsequent imposition on both of these patterns of a pneumatological understanding of the action.

We will probably never possess enough evidence to make more definitive statements about how and why baptismal anointing spread and changed, but what we do know does certainly support Bryan Spinks's caution about assuming that there was only a single line of development in any one region,[47] and especially so in Egypt and Syria. All this should discourage us from claiming in relation to modern practice that there is only one correct location in the rite for baptismal anointing and only one proper interpretation of that ceremony.

---

[45] Logan, 'Post-baptismal Chrismation in Syria'; idem, 'The Mystery of the Five Seals: Gnostic Initiation Reconsidered', *Vigiliae Christianae* 51 (1997), pp. 188–206.

[46] See *Acts of Thomas* 5, where the apostle after a meal signs his forehead, nostrils, ears, and chest with oil, apparently in preparation for a wedding.

[47] See, for example, his essay, 'Sarapion of Thmuis and Baptismal Practice in Early Christian Egypt: The Need for a Judicious Reassessment', *Worship* (1998), pp. 255–70, here at p. 259: 'this diversity may not be limited to between regions; different practices could well have existed within a region'.

Part 3
PRAYER

7

Patterns of daily praying

The consensus among liturgical scholars in the twentieth century was that prayer morning and evening formed the historical foundation of Christian practice, based on a similar pattern in Judaism, to which other hours of prayer were gradually added.[1] It also became customary to draw a distinction between what were called 'cathedral' and 'monastic' patterns of daily worship in fourth-century Christianity, a distinction which is based not simply on variations in the external forms of the worship but also on significant differences in the inner spirit expressed by those divergent forms.[2] Furthermore, the advocates of this particular classification sometimes tended to go on to suggest that what was needed in today's situation was a restoration of a 'cathedral' pattern of the daily office, in place of the essentially 'monastic' model which the churches had inherited from their medieval past. The implication of this is that the 'cathedral' tradition of the fourth century with public celebrations morning and evening was the authentic expression of Christian daily prayer and stood in direct succession to the practice of Christians in the first three centuries, while the 'monastic' tradition was a deviation from this straight line.

All of this, however, is open to question. Although the emphasis on the twofold nature of the divine office was a perfectly proper corrective to earlier scholarship, which had only been conscious of the existence of a single type – the monastic – yet in the end this simple dual classification fails to do full justice to the historical evidence, which reveals not just two but at least four different patterns of daily prayer in the early Church. Moreover, the daily devotions of the Egyptian desert ascetics and also the 'cathedral' office itself are both alike modifications of the pattern of prayer practised by Christians in earlier centuries. It is not therefore self-evident that a re-creation of the 'cathedral' model in the twenty-first

---

[1] See, for example, C. W. Dugmore, *The Influence of the Synagogue upon the Divine Office* (Oxford University Press, Oxford 1944); reprinted as Alcuin Club Collections 45 (Faith Press, London 1964).

[2] See further Paul F. Bradshaw, 'Cathedral and Monastic: What's in a Name?', *Worship* 77 (2003), pp. 341–53.

century would be the restoration of the truly authentic form of Christian worship and the panacea for all the contemporary difficulties which surround the celebration of what the Roman Catholic Church now calls the Liturgy of the Hours. Let us then review the historical evidence for these early Christian prayer practices.

Pattern 1: Daily prayer before the fourth century

The earliest references to a specific Christian pattern of daily prayer are not to one twice a day but three times. The *Didache*, probably compiled around the end of the first century, directs that the Lord's Prayer be said three times a day (8.2–3), but does not specify which particular times, presumably expecting those already to be familiar to its readers. Clement of Alexandria a century later, even though advocating the practice of constant prayer himself, also reveals familiarity with a threefold pattern of daily prayer that he says some Christians observe, and specifies the third, sixth, and ninth hours of the day as being the times for this (approximately 9 a.m., 12 noon, and 3 p.m.).[3] His compatriot Origen too, later in the third century, recommends that prayer be offered not less than three times a day and again in the night. He cites the biblical precedents of Daniel praying three times a day (Daniel 6.10), of Peter praying at the sixth hour (Acts 10.9) as an instance of the middle of the three times, of the words 'the lifting up of my hands as an evening sacrifice' (Psalm 141.2) as an instance of the third, and of the verse 'At midnight I rose to give thanks to you because of your righteous judgements' (Psalm 119.62) together with Paul and Silas praying at midnight while in prison (Acts 16.25) as instances of prayer in the night.[4] Finally, Edward Phillips has disentangled from the multi-layered text known as the *Apostolic Tradition* of Hippolytus a recommended pattern of daily prayer at the third, sixth, and ninth hours and at midnight. Phillips suggests that while some communities followed the natural rhythm of the day and performed their threefold prayer in the morning, at noon, and in the evening, others adopted the third, sixth, and ninth hours instead.[5] It may well be that these variations reflect differences between rural Christians, whose pattern was determined by the movement of the sun, and urban Christians, who would have

---

[3] Clement of Alexandria, *Stromata* 7.7.40.

[4] Origen, *De oratione* 12.2; see also *Contra Celsum* 6.41.

[5] L. Edward Phillips, 'Daily Prayer in the *Apostolic Tradition* of Hippolytus', *Journal of Theological Studies* 40 (1989), pp. 389–400. For the critical questions surrounding the *Apostolic Tradition*, see above, pp. 46–50.

heard the public announcement in cities of these major divisions of the Roman day[6] and adopted them for their prayer.

Threefold daily prayer also seems to have Jewish antecedents. Although the attempt to make prayer in the morning, the afternoon and the evening a general imposition on Jews (the first two hours being associated with what had been the times of the daily sacrifices) does not appear to have begun until well after the destruction of the Temple, there are signs that prayer three times a day, but not yet linked to the Temple hours, was being practised by some pious groups well prior to this, including those at Qumran.[7] Prayer in the night may also have been part of the Qumran cycle, but in any case would have been a natural development for Christians expecting their Lord to return 'like a thief in the night'.[8] The fact that Christians also faced east whenever they prayed, like some Jewish groups, suggests that the roots of their regular times of prayer lay in encouraging a state of constant eschatological readiness.[9]

On the other hand, the writings of the third-century North African authors Tertullian and Cyprian attest to a more developed pattern of daily prayer there. They are aware that the only absolute apostolic injunction binding upon a Christian is to 'pray without ceasing' (1 Thessalonians 5.17), but they both recommend that, in order to fulfil this, one should pray five times each day – in the morning, at the third, sixth, and ninth hours, and in the evening – and should also rise from sleep in the middle of the night to pray again. It looks as though the two versions of threefold daily prayer – prayer in the morning, at noon, and in the evening, and prayer at the third, sixth, and ninth hours – have been combined in this region to create this more extensive pattern.

Tertullian attempts to find biblical precedents for these particular times. The third, sixth, and ninth hours, he says, 'can be found in the Scriptures in established use. The Holy Spirit was first poured out on the assembled disciples at the third hour. On the day on which Peter experienced the vision of everything common in that vessel, he had ascended to the housetop at the sixth hour in order to pray. He, with John, was going up to the Temple at the ninth hour, where he restored the paralytic man

---

[6] See Tertullian, *De ieiunio* 10.

[7] See, for example, Daniel 6.10; Sarason, 'Communal Prayer at Qumran and Among the Rabbis', pp. 151–72, here at p. 157 and n. 24, and at p. 167 and nn. 64, 65.

[8] See Matthew 24.43–4; Luke 12.35–40; 1 Thessalonians 5.2–11; 2 Peter 3.10; Revelation 3.3; 16.15.

[9] Tertullian, *Apologeticum* 16; *Ad nationes* 1.13; Clement of Alexandria, *Stromata* 7.7; Origen, *De oratione* 32; cf. Josephus, *Jewish War* 2.128; Philo, *De vita contemplativa* 27, 89. See further Bradshaw, *Daily Prayer in the Early Church*, pp. 37–9, 57–9.

to health.' Tertullian goes on to admit that these are simply statements, 'without a precept of any observance', but hopes that they are sufficient to 'establish some presumption which may both enforce a command to pray and as if by law drag us from business for a while for such duty', so that 'we may worship not less than three times each day'. As he cannot find similar precedents for morning and evening prayer, he is reduced to describing them as 'our obligatory prayers, which without any command are due at the beginning of daylight and of night'.[10] He refers elsewhere to prayer in the night when raising as one of his objections to mixed marriages that a Christian wife will not be able to escape her pagan husband's notice when she rises during the night to pray.[11]

Cyprian also traces prayer at the third, sixth, and ninth hours to biblical precedents. Like Tertullian, he believes that the three times of prayer observed by Daniel were at these times, and refers also to the descent of the Spirit on the disciples at the third hour and Peter's vision at the sixth hour, but adds to these the period of Christ's crucifixion from the sixth to the ninth hour. 'But for us, dearly beloved brethren, in addition to the hours anciently observed, both the times and the symbolic aspects of praying have now increased. For prayer must be made also in the morning, so that the resurrection of the Lord may be celebrated by morning prayer . . . Likewise when the sun sets at the ending of the day it is necessary for prayer to be made again.' He goes on to affirm that there is no hour when Christians 'ought not constantly and continually to worship God', and so should not cease from prayer 'even by night'.[12]

Most scholars have sought to distinguish the status of the morning and evening hours mentioned here from the other times of prayer, and seen the former as obligatory for all Christians at the time and the latter as merely 'recommended'. However, an unbiased reading of the texts suggests rather that all the occasions for prayer referred to by writers of the period, including the night, are considered as having equal importance to one another, as means towards the fulfilment of the end, a life in constant communion with God. There is, of course, no way of knowing how many ordinary Christians actually did manage to maintain this extensive daily schedule, but it should be remembered that the initiatory practices of the Church at this period demanded a high level of commitment from those seeking admission to the faith, so that it was more akin to what we would think of as entering a religious order. Moreover, this pattern of prayer was

---

[10] Tertullian, *De oratione* 25.
[11] Tertullian, *Ad uxorem* 2.5.
[12] Cyprian, *De Dominica oratione* 34–6.

probably not felt to be quite as demanding as it appears to modern eyes. Rising in the middle of the night for prayer, for example, is not as difficult in a culture where there was little to do except sleep between sunset and sunrise and where it was common for people to wake for a while part way through the night before returning to a second period of sleep.

It is impossible to describe in detail the content of the daily prayers from this period, since there are very few extant early prayer-texts at all and none of them belong to these occasions, but from the allusions made by ancient writers it would seem that third-century Christians maintained the character, if not the form, of prayer reflected in New Testament documents, and especially the Pauline Epistles, and derived ultimately from Judaism, of praise and thanksgiving leading to petition and intercession for others.[13] Such prayer seems generally to have been offered either by individuals on their own or by small groups of family and friends and not in formal liturgical assemblies, which appear to have been limited chiefly to the celebration of the eucharist on Sundays and to services of the word at the ninth hour on Wednesdays and Fridays.

Nevertheless, this does not mean that the daily prayers were thought of as being merely private prayer. As Cyprian makes clear, each person's prayer was seen as being a participation in the prayer of the whole Church: 'Before all things the Teacher of peace and Master of unity did not wish prayer to be made singly and individually, so that when one prays, he does not pray for himself alone . . . For us prayer is public and common, and when we pray, we do not pray for one, but for the whole people, because we, the whole people, are one.'[14] Such intercession was not only for other Christians, but for the whole world: according to Tertullian, it included prayer 'for the emperors, for their ministers and for all in authority, for the welfare of the world, for the prevalence of peace, for the delay of the final consummation'.[15] Moreover, Christians also viewed their acts of prayer as a sacrifice offered to God and as the true fulfilment of the 'perpetual' (*tamid*) daily sacrifices of the Old Testament (see Exodus 29.38–42; 30.7–8; Numbers 28.3–6).[16] Here then, indeed, was the royal priesthood of the Church, though dispersed, engaged in its priestly task – continually offering the sacrifice of praise and thanksgiving to God on behalf of all creation, and interceding for the salvation of the world.

---

[13] For further details, see Bradshaw, *Daily Prayer in the Early Church*, chs 1–3.

[14] Cyprian, *De Dominica oratione* 8.

[15] Tertullian, *Apologeticum* 39; see also ibid., 30–2.

[16] See, for example, Tertullian, *De oratione* 28; Irenaeus, *Adversus haereses* 4.18.6; Origen, *Homiliae in Numerorum* 23.3; *Contra Celsum* 8.21–2.

Finally, we should note two things which were seemingly not characteristics of the hours of prayer at this time. They did not usually involve the recitation of psalms, for Tertullian tells us that the more assiduous were adding to their prayers those psalms which included an Alleluia, to which those present could make the response,[17] thereby clearly implying that other people did not. Instead the psalms were generally used in connection with community meals, whether eucharistic or not, where various individuals sang either one of the canonical psalms or a hymn of their own composition to the others.[18] Nor again did the hours of prayer generally include a ministry of the word, not because the reading of the Scriptures was not valued by the early Christians, but because this was normally done in other contexts, in the corporate assemblies for worship on Sundays, Wednesdays, and Fridays, alluded to above, and in occasional catechetical classes intended for new converts. This restriction was inevitable for purely practical reasons: when one considers the difficulty – and high cost – of providing additional copies of the Scriptures, to say nothing of the low level of literacy among many converts, it will be apparent that studying the Bible at home can only have been possible for a relatively few educated and wealthier members of the Church.

Pattern 2: The fourth-century 'cathedral' office

After the Peace of Constantine in the fourth century, when daily communal assemblies for prayer became a more realistic possibility, evidence from a variety of sources points to the conclusion that in most places they were held only twice each day, in the morning and in the evening, this choice seemingly being governed primarily by the practical problems associated with meeting together during the working day or in the middle of the night.[19] It was of course hoped that individuals and families might still continue to pray at the other hours on their own,[20] but only the exceptionally pious appear to have done so in the less disciplined environment of fourth-century Christianity. Thus daily prayer for ordinary Christians now differed in two important respects from the practice of earlier times:

---

[17] Tertullian, *De oratione* 27 (*MECL* 78).

[18] See Clement, *Stromata* 7.7; Tertullian, *Apologeticum* 39; Cyprian, *Epistula* 1.16 (*MECL* 61, 74, 94).

[19] For details of primary sources, see Robert F. Taft, *The Liturgy of the Hours in East and West* (The Liturgical Press, Collegeville 1986; 2nd edn 1993), pp. 31–56.

[20] See John Chrysostom, *Expositio in psalmum* 133; *Homiliae in Acta Apostolorum* 26; *De Anna sermo* 4.5.

it had gained more of a corporate expression but its frequency was effect-ively reduced.

Although the shift from individual to corporate praying was in one way only making explicit what had been implicit in the previous century – that Christian prayer was always the prayer of the whole Church – yet an impor-tant difference of ecclesiology underlies it and was to have significant con-sequences for the future history of daily prayer in the Church. The vision of 'church' reflected in the practice of the third century was one in which each individual was equally responsible for playing his or her part in main-taining the priestly activity of the body. This was replaced in the fourth century by a more centralized, hierarchically ordered, institutional model of the Church, still involving the whole body in prayer but with much more stress on the community than on the individual. Worship was led by a number of different ministers, each charged with a specific task – the bishop or presbyter to preside and pronounce the orations, the deacon to proclaim the biddings, the cantor to chant the verses of the psalms – and the ordinary individual was now merely one member of the congregation with no specific responsibility of his or her own. What mattered was that the Church should pray as an assembly, and the presence or absence of one person from the gathering did not significantly affect that activity. Except when it was their turn to perform one of the liturgical functions, even ordained ministers had no special obligation to be there above that of anyone else.

The corporate nature of daily prayer also gave rise to other differences in its form and character. Psalms and hymns, which (as noted above) had earlier been a characteristic of the less frequent communal meal gather-ings, now assume a central place in the daily services. Moreover, because of the increased size of the assembly and consequently the need for a more regular and formal structure, these are no longer freely chosen and sung by individual members of the community, but are now fixed and are performed by an officially appointed cantor. The psalms of praise, Psalms 148–50, seem to have become the universal core of morning prayer every day of the week, together with the canticle *Gloria in excelsis* in the East. Evening prayer appears to have a less generally accepted form: the hymn *Phos hilaron*, connected with the ceremonial lighting of the evening lamp, is widely attested in the East but not the West. Psalm 63, understood to refer to morning, and Psalm 141 with its reference to evening are also found at those hours in many Eastern rites. Even the concluding ritual seems to have undergone a transformation: whereas formerly the participants at a Christian prayer-gathering apparently exchanged a kiss with one another as 'the seal of prayer',[21] the cathedral office ends instead with an imposition of hands by the presiding minister on each of the worshippers – a further illustration of ecclesiological shift which had taken place.

Some things, however, remain constant from the prayer patterns of earlier centuries. Prayer is still considered as a sacrifice offered to God, though the twice-daily 'perpetual' sacrifices of the Old Testament are now seen as finding their fulfilment not in the ceaseless prayer of Christians but more literally in the morning and evening assemblies themselves.[22] The cathedral office still centres around the praise of God – but now expressed in a small number of psalms and hymns repeated every day – and intercession for others, though as time went by this activity tended to focus more on the needs of the Church than those of the world, perhaps because the boundaries between the two were much less obviously marked than they had been before the Peace of Constantine. And finally, the ministry of the word still does not feature in the normal daily worship but continues to be mainly restricted to the Sunday, Wednesday, and Friday assemblies, and to catechetical instruction held during Lent and Easter week.[23]

Pattern 3: The worship of the desert ascetics

There had always been some whose spirituality was not satisfied merely with frequent times of prayer during the day but who wished to fulfil more literally the apostolic injunction to 'pray without ceasing'. Such was, for example, the attitude of Clement of Alexandria,[24] and it was inherited by the desert ascetics of the early fourth century. As the Church moved out from under the risk of persecution and became socially acceptable, they found its standards becoming too lax and lacking the sort of challenge for which they were looking. They therefore took to the Egyptian and Syrian deserts in order to live a rigorous life as hermits, set apart from the rest of the Church. Their aim was to maintain as near as possible a ceaseless vigil of prayer, punctuated only by the minimal interruption for food and sleep. The semi-anchorite communities that sprang up in Lower Egypt also prayed individually in their cells during the week, assembling together only on Saturdays and Sundays. Rising very early every day, apparently at cockcrow, they worked while they prayed and prayed while they worked. With the emergence of the coenobitic life in the communities founded

---

[21] So it is described by Tertullian, *De oratione* 18.
[22] See John Chrysostom, *Expositio in psalmum* 140.3.
[23] See Bradshaw, *Daily Prayer in the Early Church*, pp. 90–2.
[24] Clement of Alexandria, *Stromata* 7.7.

by Pachomius in Upper Egypt, however, more formal rules of prayer began to be established. While still expecting the monk to persevere in praying throughout his waking hours, these prescribed two communal gatherings each day, on rising in the morning and before retiring to bed at night.[25]

Though there may be some similarity with regard to the number and times of the assemblies for daily prayer between this last institution and the cathedral office, what we have here in all the desert traditions is radically different in character from that worship, and equally a deviation from the prayer-life of Christians of earlier centuries. What is retained from the spirituality of former times is the ideal of prayer without ceasing, and the emphasis on the responsibility of each individual to engage in prayer. What is new, at least compared with the mainstream of earlier Christian prayer, is the attempt to give ceaseless prayer a more literal interpretation: whereas from New Testament times onwards Christians had viewed the whole of their life as constituting an unceasing prayer offered to God,[26] these desert ascetics, on the other hand, were determined that prayer itself should constitute the sole content of their life. As Alexander Schmemann has said, 'This is not the illumination of life and work by prayer, not a joining of these things in prayer, not even a turning of life into prayer, but prayer as life or, more properly, the replacement of life by prayer.'[27]

What is also new is the nature of the prayer in which they engaged – reflection on the mighty works of God and supplication for spiritual growth and personal salvation. The substance of the praying of these desert fathers, whether done alone or with others, seems to have been the continual alternation of the recitation of a psalm and a period of

---

[25] John Cassian in his account of Egyptian monastic practices in his *Institutes* seems to have confused the practices of Upper and Lower Egypt. As Robert Taft has indicated (*The Liturgy of the Hours in East and West*, p. 58), Cassian was not simply writing as a disinterested observer: he was using the example of the Egyptian monks as an ideal to promote a reform of monasticism in his native Gaul. Hence, discrepancies between his description and evidence obtained from other sources may be signs of a desire to furnish Egyptian precedents for those Gallican practices which he favoured, and so his testimony needs to be treated with great caution. In particular, his claim that 12 psalms were recited each morning and evening cannot be accepted uncritically as the original practice. Instead, this appears to have its roots in a tradition that 12 prayers be offered each day and 12 each night, in other words that one should pray at every hour or constantly. Thus the grouping of these prayers into two daily synaxes of 12 psalms each seems to be a later development: see Taft, *The Liturgy of the Hours in East and West*, p. 72; Veilleux, *La liturgie dans le cénobitisme pâchomien au IVe siècle*, pp. 324–39.

[26] See, for example, Romans 12.1; 1 Corinthians 10.31; Origen, *De oratione* 12.2.

[27] Alexander Schmemann, *Introduction to Liturgical Theology* (Faith Press, London/American Orthodox Press, Portland, ME 1966), p. 107.

meditation.[28] The twice-daily assemblies in Pachomian monasticism involved a similar alternation, but here consisting of a series of biblical
passages read aloud by one of the brothers while the rest listened and engaged
in silent prayer between each one; only on Sunday mornings were psalms
sung.[29] Now of course remembrance, *anamnesis*, of what God had done
in Christ had always been central to Christian prayer, but here it took
on a somewhat different character. Mainstream Christianity had recalled
God's works in order to offer praise and thanks for them, whereas the
primary purpose of the extended meditation here was formation: the monk
meditated on the Scriptures, and especially the psalms, in order to grow
into the likeness of Christ,[30] and prayed for the requisite grace for that
growth. Like the movement towards more truly ceaseless praying, this again
is something with its roots in the early Alexandrian tradition, which, while
not denying the legitimacy or efficacy of intercession, regarded petition
for spiritual rather than material gifts as the higher way. Monastic rules
obliging monks to engage in prayer at certain prescribed hours or to
say a particular number of psalms and prayers, therefore, sprang from
what might be called a pedagogical rather than a liturgical motive: it was
designed to further ascetical growth towards what was thought of as
'spiritual freedom'.

Although it has to be admitted that formation is necessarily involved
in all liturgy, and regular participation in any rite has a significant effect
upon individual spiritual development, yet by making it the principal
aim of daily prayer rather than a secondary by-product, the Egyptian
monastic tradition seriously distorted the nature of the activity and led
to an impoverishment and narrowing of its focus. Since such prayer
was essentially individualistic, it obscured and lost sight of the ecclesial
dimension which had implicitly undergirded the prayer-life of early
Christians. Whereas prayer on one's own had been the result of necessity
in earlier times, this was not so for those who had voluntarily withdrawn
to the desert. It was the same prayer which was performed in the cell as
in the community gathering, and neither setting was seen as superior
to the other. There was nothing inherently corporate in the worship,

---

[28] On this, see further below, pp. 119–20. Frans Kok, 'L'office pachômien: *psallere, orare, legere*', *Ecclesia Orans* 9 (1992), pp. 69–95, challenged the scholarly consensus and argued that the daily services did include psalmody in addition to other biblical readings and prayer, but he has not won support for his position.

[29] See Veilleux, *La liturgie dans le cénobitisme pâchomien au IVe siècle*, pp. 307–15; Taft, *The Liturgy of the Hours in East and West*, pp. 62–5.

[30] On this, see below, p. 118.

nothing which might not be done equally as well alone as together. Although a communal assembly offered an element of mutual encouragement in the work of prayer, and afforded opportunity for supervision and discipline over the possible weakness and indolence of the more junior brethren, nevertheless the presence or absence of other people was ultimately a matter of indifference.[31]

Not only did the ecclesial dimension disappear from prayer, so too did what might be called the cosmic dimension. Whereas earlier Christians had been very conscious of their mission towards the whole world and so concerned to pray for all God's creation, prayer here became orientated inwards instead of outwards. The monk's primary responsibility was towards his own soul and not the salvation of others. In other words, the sense of a vocation to the royal priesthood of the Church had been eroded. For, as J. G. Davies has observed, a priesthood is

> never established for itself, so that for the royal priesthood to celebrate its *own* cultus for its *own* needs is to deny its very *raison d'être*; it would cease in fact to function as a priesthood. An introverted cultus performed by the covenant people is therefore a contradiction of their office, a rejection of their commission and a failure to participate in the *missio Dei*. It makes nonsense of the whole idea of covenant and priesthood. This means that only a cultus which is outward-looking and related to the world can be regarded as an authentic act of Christian worship. If it is not worldly, in this sense, then Christians are not exercising their baptismal priesthood.[32]

From all this it can easily be seen why it came to be thought vitally important that each individual fulfilled personally whatever was prescribed in the community's rule. It was not enough, for example, that the rest of the community maintained a regular time of prayer on rising each morning: if the individual did not participate in it, then he would derive no spiritual benefit from it. Nor did it particularly matter if he said this prayer earlier or later than the rest of the community: as long as he did it at some point, he would still have fulfilled his duty. Here then lie the roots of the idea that missed prayer can somehow be 'made up' at a later time, that what matters is that the work should eventually be done by each individual, rather than that the body of the Church should remain in constant communion with God through a regular cycle of prayer-times.

Finally, one other important new development in this tradition needs to be noted, and this is the use of the Psalter, the whole Psalter, and almost

---

[31] See Taft, *The Liturgy of the Hours in East and West*, pp. 66–73.
[32] J. G. Davies, *Worship and Mission* (SCM Press, London 1966), p. 95.

nothing but the Psalter in the daily devotions. As we shall see in greater detail in the next chapter, there is no evidence to suggest that any more than certain selected psalms, mainly those in which Christological prophecy could easily be seen and/or which expressed praise and invited the response 'Alleluia', were ever used in early Christian worship, and certainly nothing to support the notion that the whole Psalter was read through in its entirety. Similarly, there is no evidence of the widespread use of psalms in Jewish worship, or of any preference for these canonical texts over contemporary compositions either in more informal Jewish gatherings or in similar Christian assemblies.[33] The claim frequently made, therefore, that in saying the psalms we are praying the prayers that Jesus himself used, lacks any sure foundation.

The use of the psalms in the prayer-life of the desert ascetics, on the other hand, stands in sharp contrast to this. Here the Psalter was elevated to the place of honour in religious formation: the novice was expected to learn the whole Psalter by heart, and it came to be regarded as a great and worthy accomplishment to recite all 150 psalms in the space of twenty-four hours.[34] There seem to be several reasons to account for this striking development. First, because of their supposed Davidic authorship the psalms were regarded as especially inspired: they were 'the songs of the Spirit', in contrast to ecclesiastical compositions, which were dismissed as 'the words of mere mortals'.[35] This attitude was greatly encouraged by the fact that at the time hymns were often used as a means of spreading and popularizing heretical beliefs.[36] Second, the tradition of Christological interpretation[37] made them particularly attractive to those who were attempting to form their lives into the pattern of Christ: what better way was there to become more Christlike than to meditate on the words of the psalms, and allow their sentiments to shape one's spirituality? Third, since the whole of life needed to be filled with such meditation, then more than just a small selection of psalms was required. Finally, since time and seasons were of no consequence, but only eternity mattered, there was no reason to try to arrange the psalms according

---

[33] See James W. McKinnon, 'On the Question of Psalmody in the Ancient Synagogue', *Early Music History* 6 (1986), pp. 159–91 = idem, *The Temple, the Church Fathers and Early Western Chant* (Ashgate, Aldershot 1998), VIII; and below, pp. 122–3.

[34] See Joseph Dyer, 'The Psalms in Monastic Prayer', in Nancy Van Deusen (ed.), *The Place of the Psalms in the Intellectual Culture of the Middle Ages* (SUNY Press, Albany, NY 1999), pp. 59–89, here at pp. 59–60.

[35] See Joseph Gelineau, 'Les psaumes à l'époque patristique', *La Maison-Dieu* 135 (1978), pp. 99–116.

[36] For the use of hymns by Arians, see Socrates, *Historia ecclesiastica* 6.8 (*MECL* 218).

[37] On this tradition, see further below, p. 118.

to their appropriateness to specific hours and occasions, and they were thus recited in their biblical order.[38]

Pattern 4: The prayer of urban ascetics

Not everyone who wanted to live a rigorous and disciplined spiritual life in the more relaxed Christian environment of the fourth century retreated to the desert. Pious individuals approached bishops and other Christian leaders for an appropriate pattern of prayer that they might practise while continuing their daily life in the cities of the Roman empire,[39] and ascetic communities also began to be formed within urban settings in Cappadocia, Syria, and elsewhere, who again sought a rule of life from their bishop. Their cycle of prayer has often been treated merely as a variant of Egyptian monasticism. This, however, is misleading, for its foundation is quite different. These individuals and groups usually prayed early in the morning; at the third, sixth, and ninth hours; in the evening; and again at some point in the night. Those living together in communities generally prayed in common (and in some cases might even join with the local church for certain hours), but they could also observe the times of prayer individually if circumstances prevented a corporate assembly.[40] Moreover, unlike Egyptian monasticism, they did not dispense with all outward ceremonial: as Gregory of Nyssa reveals in his moving account of the death of his sister Macrina, the lighting of the evening lamp with its prayer still formed a part of the daily ritual of her religious community.[41] This pattern is thus the direct descendant of the Christian prayer of the third century, and in particular of the more extended daily cycle first attested in North Africa. While the cathedral office had moved away from this pattern in one direction and the desert monks in another, these communities had persevered in the old family prayers of former

---

[38] Stig Simeon R. Frøgshov in a recent article, 'The Cathedral–Monastic Distinction Revisited, Part I: Was Egyptian Desert Liturgy a Pure Monastic Office?', *Studia Liturgica* 37 (2007), pp. 198–216, has tried to argue that such a thing as a pure monastic office with the recitation of psalms in a consecutive manner never actually existed but is the creation of modern scholars. However, the evidence for the use of selected rather than consecutive psalmody in early Egyptian monastic offices that he cites to support his case comes from a somewhat later period, when developments and changes to the original pattern had very likely taken place, and (as he himself admits) from an urban rather than a desert context, even if it subsequently spread to the latter.

[39] See, for example, Jerome, *Epistulae* 22.37; 107.9; 130.15.

[40] For details, see Bradshaw, *Daily Prayer in the Early Church*, pp. 99–106; Taft, *The Liturgy of the Hours in East and West*, pp. 75–91.

[41] Gregory of Nyssa, *Vita Macrinae* 22, 25.

times: they were not innovators, but conservatives in a world which had changed.

On the other hand, it has to be admitted that the spirituality of the desert fathers had considerable influence on them as they developed, and in most of the sources available to us a substantial vigil for a part of the night is included in their daily pattern, either appended to midnight prayer or beginning at cockcrow and lasting until the morning office.[42] This, however, seems to be a secondary addition to the cycle, and is not part of the Cappadocian pattern outlined by Basil of Caesarea: the vigil he describes appears to be an occasional event rather than a regular daily night office.[43] Chrysostom implies that the element of intercession for others in the daily services also gave way to prayer for personal spiritual progress, no doubt again under the influence of the same source: 'They ask nothing of things present, for they have no regard for these, but that they may stand with boldness before the fearful judgement-seat . . . and that no one may hear the fearful voice that saith, "I know you not", and that with a pure conscience and many good deeds they may pass through this toilsome life and sail over the angry sea with a favourable wind.'[44]

The evidence suggests, however, that, with the exception of their extended prayer in the night and a weekly all-night vigil,[45] such communities were conservative in their use of psalmody, and at first continued to employ a selective rather than a consecutive approach in their other hours of prayer. The remains of this can still be detected even in later Western monastic rules, where the Egyptian way of praying was more extensively imitated than in the East, strongly encouraged by Cassian's idealization of it. Indeed, while the cathedral tradition had developed communal refrains appropriate to each psalm, the monastic tradition originally tended to adhere to the more primitive custom of the Alleluia response alone, and did not restrict this to the Easter season as ecclesiastical usage came to do.

Conclusion

As I indicated at the beginning, it has become fashionable to regard the 'cathedral' office as the normative expression of early Christian prayer,

---

[42] Pseudo-Athanasius, *De virginitate* 20; John Chrysostom, *Homiliae in epistulam I ad Timotheum* 14.4; John Cassian, *De institutis coenobiorum* 3.4–6.

[43] Basil, *Sermo asceticus* 4; *Regulae fusius tractatae* 37.3–5; *Epistulae* 2; 207.2–4. See Bradshaw, *Daily Prayer in the Early Church*, pp. 99–102; Taft, *The Liturgy of the Hours in East and West*, pp. 39–41, 84–7.

[44] John Chrysostom, *Homiliae in Matthaeum* 68.3; ET from *NPNF*, First Series, 10:400.

[45] For the latter, see Bradshaw, *Daily Prayer in the Early Church*, pp. 89–90.

and as the model for today's Church to follow. Our review of the evidence, however, has attempted to show that the former is not the case. The 'cathedral' office was but one development among others in the fourth century, continuing the traditions of earlier times in some respects but modifying them significantly in others. It is not self-evident, therefore, that it constitutes the ideal form which should necessarily be imitated today; and indeed there are grounds for questioning its appropriateness for many modern situations. It is formal in style and for its celebration requires a community which is able to assemble together regularly every single day, with a number of ministries represented in each assembly – bishop or presbyter, deacon, cantor. However fine this might be as a liturgical expression of the nature of the Church, relatively few Christians today find themselves in a situation where such is a real possibility. For the great majority, the 'cathedral' office is something which can only be celebrated occasionally, usually just on Sundays and festivals. It does nothing to meet the need for a pattern of *daily* praying.

For that, I would submit, we would do better to look to the pattern evidenced in the third century and continued to a large extent in the urban monastic communities of the fourth century onwards. Here we have a much more informal style of prayer, which is best done communally, but can also be performed individually if necessity dictates. It does not single out morning and evening as *the* occasions when one ought to pray, but simply emphasizes the desirability of frequent prayer at whatever times that is possible. Nor does it require the presence of ordained ministers for its celebration: in the monastic gatherings the leader of the community (who was not ordained) generally presided and said the orations – as the head of the household had done in Jewish and early Christian domestic prayer – and each member of the community took an equal turn in chanting the verses of the various psalms to the others. The only documented exception to this is in fourth-century Jerusalem, where, according to the pilgrim Egeria, presbyters and deacons were required to attend the monastic night office in order to pronounce the orations after the psalms,[46] although some unease about usurping what had come to be seen as the episcopal and presbyteral prerogative of extemporizing prayer in a communal setting also seems to have been felt in other places, and hence the recitation of the Lord's Prayer was used there instead of a collect at the end of the services.[47] The prayer of the small group, therefore, is not

---

[46] Egeria, *Itinerarium* 24.1.
[47] See, for example, Adalbert de Vogüé, *La Règle de Saint Benoît*, 5, Sources chrétiennes 185 (Éditions du Cerf, Paris 1971), pp. 493–4.

merely a more practical alternative to the 'cathedral' office, but also witnesses itself to some important truths about the nature of Christian prayer. It testifies that the prayer of the Church is not restricted to certain fixed hours and forms, however valuable they may be, but that the only absolute rule is to live a life of communion with God, punctuated by specific moments of prayer, whenever and wherever possible. It also testifies that prayer in the name of the Church is not confined to certain deputed individuals, but that on the contrary every member has both the privilege and the duty of acting as prayer-leader on behalf of others.

On the other hand, it is not without its dangers, as the history of monastic prayer shows. The Egyptian model exercised an increasingly powerful influence upon it, and still continues to shape much of the spirituality of the daily office today. Monastic communities rapidly came to adopt a cursus of psalmody which, one way or another, sought to incorporate the whole Psalter in worship, and meditation on the psalms with petition for spiritual growth replaced the praise of God and intercession for the world which were characteristic of the older concept of prayer. The absence of any liturgical expression of the ecclesial nature of the act of praying also encouraged individualism and an excessive stress on the obligation and need of each person to perform the full pensum of prayer.

This style of prayer, therefore, does need to be counter-balanced by the 'cathedral' office, for both have something significant to contribute to Christian prayer-life. For instance, the 'cathedral' office stands as a reminder to us that, because we are sharing in the Church's prayer, we are never really on our own when we pray, and even on occasions when we may be unable to participate in prayer ourselves, the Church's work of prayer still goes on, and does not remain for us to have to 'make up' at some later time. Above all, it reminds us of the kind of praying that we are called to do: it is the prayer of the Church, the royal priesthood, participating in the prayer of Christ, the great high-priest, offering the sacrifice of praise and interceding for the salvation of all. However valuable meditation on the psalms and other portions of Scripture might be as a means of stimulating and feeding our prayer, it should never be allowed to displace that primary focus.

8

The changing role of psalmody

Although psalms have played a major part in traditional Christian worship, many modern worshippers appear to be very uncertain what it is they are supposed to be doing when they say or sing them in church services. However, when we turn to the traditions of the early Church for some illumination of this question, we do not find there a single consistent apology for the Christian use of psalms, nor an unchanging practice. Instead, a number of quite different ways of using the psalms can be seen, together with their individual explanations for the particular custom. While some of these appear to have emerged in parallel with one another, others seem to have developed out of earlier forms of psalmody. This evolution in practice and interpretation over the centuries brought about a significant shift in the role that psalms played in Christian liturgy and spirituality, which we shall attempt to trace.

Psalms as prophecy

The book of Psalms is cited more frequently in the New Testament than any other Old Testament Scripture, and it is there chiefly viewed as being a book of prophecy – or one might say as *the* prophetic work *par excellence* of the Old Testament – thought to have been written by King David under the inspiration of the Holy Spirit. Thus, for example, Jesus himself is said to have cited Psalm 110.1 as a messianic prophecy:

> How can the scribes say that the Christ is the son of David? David himself, inspired by the Holy Spirit, declared:
>
> > 'The Lord said to my Lord,
> > Sit at my right hand,
> > until I put your enemies under your feet.'
>
> David himself calls him Lord; so how is he his son?[1]

---

[1] Mark 12.35–7; parallels in Matthew 22.42–5; Luke 20.41–4.

Similarly, in the Acts of the Apostles, Peter refers in his speech on the day of Pentecost (Acts 2.14–36) both to that same psalm text and also to Psalm 16.8–11 as messianic prophecies fulfilled in Jesus Christ.

This same prophetic/Christological method of interpreting psalms was continued by Christian theologians and preachers in the succeeding centuries. Among early examples is Justin Martyr's *Dialogue with Trypho*, which features an extensive treatment of Psalm 22.[2] But it was from the third century onwards, apparently under the influence of the exegetical method adopted by Origen from classical literature,[3] that Christological interpretation was gradually extended from certain selected psalms to encompass virtually all the psalms. The words of the psalms were understood either as addressed by the Church to Christ, or as speaking about Christ, or as the voice of the Christ himself. Indeed, even those texts that referred explicitly to God were commonly interpreted as really meaning the divine Christ.[4]

In the light of the above, we might well expect that at least certain psalms – or parts of psalms – that were easily susceptible of a messianic interpretation would have been used in early Christian assemblies as prophetic readings, like the other books of the Old Testament. Traces of such a custom can perhaps be seen in Luke 24.44 (where Jesus says that 'everything written about me in the law of Moses and the prophets and the psalms must be fulfilled') and in the third-century Syrian *Didascalia Apostolorum*, where the paschal vigil is said to have taken place 'with readings from the prophets, and with the Gospels and with psalms' (5.19.1). However, the meaning of both of these passages has been challenged. Some scholars have argued that the Lukan text is using the term 'psalms' in a broader sense to refer to the 'Writings', the third of the traditional Jewish divisions of the Old Testament along with the Law and the Prophets.[5] It has also been noted that the description of the paschal vigil does not say explicitly that the psalms were being used there as readings, still less as

---

[2] Justin Martyr, *Dialogue with Trypho* 97–106. For other examples, see Graham W. Woolfenden, 'The Use of the Psalter by Early Monastic Communities', *Studia Patristica* 26 (1993), pp. 88–94, here at p. 89.

[3] See Marie-Josèphe Rondeau, *Les commentaires patristiques du Psautier (IIIe–Ve siècles)*, II, Orientalia Christiana Analecta 220 (Pontificium Institutum Studiorum Orientalium, Rome 1985), pp. 39ff.

[4] The classic study of this phenomenon in early Christianity is Balthasar Fischer, 'Christ in the Psalms', *Theology Digest* 1 (1951), pp. 53–7. On the later interpretation of the psalms in the monastic tradition, see Dyer, 'The Psalms in Monastic Prayer', pp. 65ff.

[5] See, for example, Roger Beckwith, *The Old Testament Canon of the New Testament Church* (SPCK, London 1985), pp. 110–18.

prophetic readings.[6] On the other hand, somewhat more sure is the statement in the diary of the fourth-century pilgrim Egeria that at Jerusalem on Good Friday the readings were 'all about the things that Jesus suffered: first the psalms on this subject, then the Apostles which concern it, then passages from the Gospels. Thus they read the prophecies about what the Lord would suffer, and the Gospels about what he did suffer.'[7]

Since this evidence is so limited, we have no way of knowing whether the psalms might have had a place in every formal ministry of the word alongside other prophetic readings from the Old Testament in the first three centuries, or whether they were only used occasionally in place of such readings, or whether indeed they only featured once a year in connection with the paschal celebration. Our only other explicit reference to psalms in a formal ministry of the word during this period occurs in a description by Tertullian of a Montanist service led by a woman.[8] While the same practice may also have existed in the Catholic tradition of the day, we cannot automatically conclude that this was so, nor even that by the word 'psalms' Tertullian here necessarily means biblical psalms, since the term tended to be used quite loosely by patristic writers.

Psalms as the summary of Scripture

It was among the ascetics and early monastic communities of the fourth century, and especially those in the Egyptian desert, that the canonical psalms came to be used extensively within daily worship. As we saw in the previous chapter, although the early Pachomian communities of Upper Egypt read passages from a variety of biblical books and did not give any special place to the psalms in their daily services, the desert fathers in general singled out the Psalter from the rest of the Scriptures and encouraged their followers to commit its contents to memory and recite it constantly throughout their waking hours. Several of their sayings tell of individuals completing the whole Psalter in the course of a single night.[9] While such stories certainly go far beyond normal practice, they clearly illustrate the ideal towards which the serious Christian ascetic was expected to strive.

---

[6] See J. D. Crichton, *Christian Celebration: The Prayer of the Church* (Chapman, London 1976), p. 60.

[7] Egeria, *Itinerarium* 37.5; ET from Wilkinson, *Egeria's Travels*, p. 137.

[8] Tertullian, *De anima* 9.4 (*MECL* 82).

[9] See, for example, *Apophthegmata patrum*, Epiphanius 3; Serapion 1; Anonymous 150 (*MECL* 124, 126, 127).

It has sometimes been thought that the psalms were here functioning as a form of prayer. But that is not the case. The sources frequently speak of prayer *and* psalmody, and reveal that the characteristic way of using the psalms in this tradition was to alternate the saying of a psalm with a period of silent prayer. When two or more people prayed together, only one of them said the psalm and the other(s) listened to it. Then all prayed in silence, and after that another psalm was said, and so on. Thus the psalm was functioning not as prayer itself, but as a reading, as the source of inspiration for the meditative prayer that was to follow it.[10] This was true not only of the Egyptian tradition but also of ascetic practice in Syria. For example, Theodoret of Cyrrhus describes how Julian of Abiadene (*c.*350) instructed his disciples 'to go out at dawn into the desert in pairs, and while one was to offer the worship due to the Master on his knees, the other was to chant fifteen psalms of David standing; and then they were to alternate the work, the one standing to chant, the other kneeling on the ground to worship. And they continued doing this from early morning until evening.'[11]

Why those who took to the deserts should have shown such an overwhelming preference for psalms above all other Scripture for this purpose has been a source of puzzlement for scholars. But perhaps the answer lies in the prophetic/Christological interpretation described earlier. As is well known, Origen's ideas exercised a strong influence over the spirituality of the desert fathers, and hence it is likely that his Christological exegesis of the psalms would have commended itself to the early ascetics, whose fundamental aim was to conform their lives to the pattern of Christ. What better way could there be to do that, therefore, than by meditating upon the mind of Christ as revealed in the psalms?

Yet, whatever the original cause for their adoption, the psalms soon came to be regarded in this tradition as much more than Christological prophecy. The Psalter was thought to 'embrace all Scripture',[12] to encapsulate all that the rest of the Old Testament had to offer. And the monk was expected to apply its words to his life and view them as fulfilled in him.[13] This idea soon spread far outside monastic circles. Because virtually every outstanding Christian personality of the period had lived as a monk at one time or another during their career, the form of spiritual life that they advocated to ordinary lay people was essentially monastic in character. While

---

[10] See further Adalbert de Vogüé, 'Psalmodier n'est pas prier', *Ecclesia Orans* 6 (1989), pp. 7–32.

[11] Theodoret of Cyrrhus, *Historia religiosa* 2.5.

[12] A saying of Abba Philimon, in G. E. H. Palmer, P. Sherard, and K. Ware (eds), *The Philokalia* (Faber & Faber, London 1979), II, p. 347.

[13] See John Cassian, *Conferences* 10.11; Athanasius, *Epistula ad Marcellinum* 11.

these figures certainly continued to acknowledge the prophetic dimension of the Psalter,[14] they made much greater claims for it, asserting it to be a summary of all Christian teaching and the remedy for all spiritual ills. St Basil typifies the attitudes of his contemporaries:

> Now the Prophets teach some things, the Historians other things, the Law still other things, and the form of advice of the Proverbs something else, but the Book of Psalms encompasses what is valuable from them all. It prophesies what is to come; it recalls history; it legislates for life; it gives practical advice; and it is in general a common treasury of good teachings, carefully finding what is suitable for each person. For it heals the old wounds of souls; it brings swift recovery to the recently wounded; it treats what is diseased; it preserves what is pure; and as far as possible it takes away the passions that in many ways dominate souls in the life of human beings. And it does this with a certain diligent persuasion and sweetness that engender a moderate disposition.[15]

The Christian leaders who viewed the Psalter from this perspective did not lose sight of the fact that the psalms were hymnic in form. Indeed, they could hardly do so, since (as we shall see below) psalms were being sung as hymns in the church services that they themselves attended. But they still argued that the teaching function was primary, and that God had deliberately arranged matters in this way in order to make learning more pleasurable for human beings:

> When the Holy Spirit saw that the human race was with difficulty led toward virtue, and that because of our inclination toward pleasure we neglected an upright life, what did he do? He mixed sweetness of melody with the teachings so that by the pleasantness and softness of the sound heard we might receive without realizing it the benefit of the words, just like wise physicians, who often smear the cup with honey when giving the fastidious rather bitter medicines to drink. Therefore he devised these harmonious melodies of the psalms for us, so that those who are children in age or even those who are young in their ways might appear to be singing but in reality be training their souls.[16]

---

[14] See, for some examples, Pierre Salmon, *The Breviary through the Centuries* (The Liturgical Press, Collegeville 1962), pp. 42–61.

[15] Basil of Caesarea, *Homilia in psalmum* 1.1. For other examples see Ambrose, *Explanatio psalmi* 1.7, 9; Athanasius, *Epistula ad Marcellinum*; John Chrysostom, *Expositio in psalmum* 41.1; Niceta of Remesiana, *De psalmodiae bono* 5. See also Brian Daley, 'Finding the Right Key: The Aims and Strategies of Early Christian Interpretation of the Psalms', in Harold W. Attridge and Margot E. Fassler (eds), *Psalms in Community* (SBL, Atlanta 2003), pp. 189–205.

[16] Basil, *Homilia in psalmum* 1.1. See also John Chrysostom, *Expositio in psalmum* 41.1; *Homiliae in epistulam ad Colossenses* 9.2; Niceta of Remesiana, *De psalmodiae bono* 5.

Of the fourth-century advocates of psalmody, only Athanasius, who in any case belonged to a slightly older generation than the others, dissented from this latter explanation: 'Some of the simple ones among us, even while believing the texts to be divinely inspired, still think that the psalms are sung melodiously for the sake of good sound and the pleasure of the ear. This is not so.' Instead, in typical Alexandrian fashion, he adopted an allegorical explanation for the use of chant: 'to recite the psalms with melody is not done from a desire for pleasing sound, but is a manifestation of harmony among the thoughts of the soul. And melodious reading is a sign of the well-ordered and tranquil condition of the mind.'[17]

Psalms as hymns

At the same time as psalms were in the ascendancy in desert monasticism, a small number of them were also finding a place within the 'cathedral' office that was emerging after the Peace of Constantine.[18] However, their inclusion here was not derived from the monastic custom, since they had an entirely different function and method of execution. They are explicitly described as 'hymns', and performed in a quite distinct manner: after each verse chanted by a cantor, the assembly repeated a refrain, and there was apparently no period of silence after the psalm.

This practice was not a complete innovation of the fourth century. Tertullian at the beginning of the third century informs us that 'those who are more diligent in praying are accustomed to include in their prayers Alleluia and this type of psalms, with the ending of which those who are present may respond' (*De oratione* 27). Biblical psalms had also been included along with non-canonical compositions that were sung by individuals to others at mealtimes: Tertullian again states that at the end of a Christian community supper 'after the washing of hands and the lighting of lamps, each is invited to stand in the middle and sing a hymn to God, from the holy Scriptures or of his own composition as he is able'.[19] This usage may very well be the source of the later adoption of psalms in other occasions of corporate prayer, in the same way that the ritual lighting of the lamp was taken over into the evening office of the 'cathedral' tradition from earlier Christian communal meals.

---

[17] Athanasius, *Epistula ad Marcellinum* 27, 29; ET from *MECL* 100.

[18] See above, pp. 107–8.

[19] Tertullian, *Apologeticum* 39.18. This custom also continued in later centuries: see, for example, John Chrysostom, *Expositio in psalmum* 41.2 (*MECL* 166).

Singing psalms and hymns in connection with meals was certainly very ancient. The Jewish writer Philo of Alexandria, in recounting the customs of a sectarian community known as the Therapeutae, describes their practice in similar terms to Tertullian. At their festal meals 'the president rises and sings a hymn addressed to God, either a new one which he has composed or an ancient one by poets of old . . . After him the others take their turn in the order in which they are arranged, while all the rest listen in complete silence, except when they have to chant the closing lines and refrains, for then they all, men and women, sing . . .'[20] In the New Testament 1 Corinthians 14.26 includes a 'psalm' among the verbal contributions that individual participants might bring to a Christian ministry of the word, and Ephesians 5.19 speaks of believers 'addressing one another in psalms and hymns and spiritual songs . . .'. Both of these occasions may well have been in connection with a meal.[21] We cannot of course be sure that canonical psalms were included in these last two instances as well as psalms and hymns composed by Christians themselves, but it seems likely that they were, given the high regard for the psalms displayed by the New Testament writers.

It appears probable, therefore, that the use of psalms as hymns has its roots in the use of psalms as prophecy. Individual first-century Christians would have sung selected Old Testament psalms to demonstrate that Christ was the expected Messiah, having fulfilled what had been prophesied in the Scriptures, and the assembled community would have responded to each verse with an acclamation of praise. Yet by the time that we are in a position to identify the particular psalms being sung as hymns in the fourth-century 'cathedral' office, any former connection with the prophetic usage must have been lost along the way. It is not the obviously Christological ones that constitute the regular core here, but instead psalms inviting praise which include within them the Alleluia response (Psalms 148–50), and also those appropriate to the particular hour of the day (e.g., 63 in the morning, 141 in the evening).

Nevertheless, the use of the responsorial method of psalmody clearly implies an affiliation to the two preceding uses that we have examined. Although they were called 'hymns', it was actually the refrain, and not the psalm itself, that constituted the song of praise to God. The psalm verses

---

[20] Philo, *De vita contemplativa* 80. See also Peter Jeffery, 'Philo's Impact on Christian Psalmody', in Attridge and Fassler (eds), *Psalms in Community*, pp. 147–87.
[21] See Bradshaw, *Daily Prayer in the Early Church*, pp. 44–5.

were still apparently viewed as the word of God, since they are pro-claimed by one voice alone to the listening assembly. And Augustine can on occasion refer to the responsorial psalm in the eucharistic ministry of the word as a 'reading'.[22] Of course, one might want to argue that, in the absence of printed texts and in any case in a culture in which there was a large measure of illiteracy, the responsorial method was the only practical way to use unfamiliar liturgical texts. But, while this may be true, we need to remember that the psalms employed in the 'cathedral' office were very few in number and were generally repeated every single day throughout the year. The problem of unfamiliarity therefore cannot have lasted for long, and does not really explain the universal adherence to this method of psalm-singing.

Moreover, John Chrysostom offers an explanation of the significance of the refrain that supports this conclusion: 'Do not then think that you have come here simply to say the words, but when you make the response, consider that response to be a covenant. For when you say, "Like the hart desires the watersprings, my soul desires you, O God", you make a covenant with God. You have signed a contract without paper or ink; you have confessed with your voice that you love him more than all, that you prefer nothing to him, and that you burn with love for him . . .'[23]

Psalmody as praise

We have suggested that a distinction should be drawn between the use of psalms in Egyptian desert spirituality, where the whole Psalter was recited in its biblical order as the basis for individual meditation, and the use in the fourth-century 'cathedral' office, where selected psalms were sung by a cantor as a proclamation of God's word, to which the community responded with a refrain expressing their praise of God. This distinction, however, rapidly became blurred, and in later centuries disappeared altogether, with the result that in both monastic and secular circles in the West the chanting of psalms came to be thought of as itself an act of praise to God.

James McKinnon described the roots of this development as a 'psalmodic movement', which he defined as 'an unprecedented wave of enthusiasm for the singing of psalms that spread from east to west

---

[22] Augustine, *Sermones* 165; 176. On the origin of this psalm in the eucharist, see James W. McKinnon, 'The Fourth-Century Origin of the Gradual', *Early Music History* 7 (1987), pp. 91–106 = idem, *The Temple, the Church Fathers and Early Western Chant*, IX.

[23] John Chrysostom, *Expositio in psalmum* 41.5.

through the Christian population in the closing decades of the fourth century'.[24] He attributed the source of this movement to the influence of desert monasticism. While the idea of using the whole Psalter certainly came from there, Joseph Dyer has rightly qualified his claim and argued that it was in urban monastic circles that the *singing* of the psalms was fostered and developed, as a distrust of music as being a distraction to monastic values was common among the desert fathers.[25] McKinnon attributed the shaping of the 'cathedral' office itself to monasticism: 'it is no exaggeration to say that the urban ecclesiastical office, the so-called cathedral office, was flooded with the continuous psalmody of monasticism'.[26] But this does seem to be something of an exaggeration. Once again, as we saw in the preceding chapter, it was in urban monasticism that continuous psalmody was first introduced alongside selective psalmody, and it was their hybrid practice, rather than the pure 'cathedral' office as such, that became the foundation for the worship patterns of virtually all later forms of the daily office.[27]

The mingling of the two traditions in urban monasticism effectively obscured the previous contrast between the psalms as Scripture and selected psalms as hymns, and caused leading church figures of the fourth century both to advocate the use of much more extensive psalmody by ordinary Christians and to offer explanations for its dual function, as we noted earlier. It also, in turn, encouraged these monastic communities to take greater cognizance of the hymnic character of the psalms and to

---

[24] James W. McKinnon, 'Desert Monasticism and the Later Fourth-Century Psalmodic Movement', *Music and Letters* 75 (1994), pp. 505–21, here at p. 506 = idem, *The Temple, the Church Fathers and Early Western Chant*, XI. See also idem, 'The Book of Psalms, Monasticism, and the Western Liturgy', in Van Deusen (ed.), *The Place of the Psalms in the Intellectual Culture of the Middle Ages*, pp. 43–58.

[25] Joseph Dyer, 'The Desert, the City and Psalmody in the Late Fourth Century', in Sean Gallagher (ed.), *Western Plainchant in the First Millennium* (Ashgate, Aldershot 2003), pp. 11–43, esp. pp. 21–4. For urban monasticism, see above, pp. 113–14; and for the reluctance of desert monks to accept liturgical chant, see Robert F. Taft, 'Christian Liturgical Psalmody: Origins, Development, Decomposition, Collapse', in Attridge and Fassler (eds), *Psalms in Community*, pp. 7–32, here at pp. 12–14.

[26] McKinnon, 'The Book of Psalms, Monasticism, and the Western Liturgy', pp. 50–1. Peter Jeffery concurred with him: 'Monastic Reading and the Emerging Roman Chant Repertory', in Gallagher (ed.), *Western Plainchant in the First Millennium*, pp. 45–103, here at pp. 47–8.

[27] The phenomenon of the 'popular psalmodic vigil' that McKinnon particularly cites to support his claim for the influence of monasticism on the 'cathedral' office, although certainly having its origins among ordinary Christians in earlier centuries, appears rather to have become something that was kept alive from the fourth century onwards only by urban monastics and those exceptionally pious individuals who supported them, and not by the general Christian populace. See below, p. 139 and Dyer, 'The Desert, the City and Psalmody in the Late Fourth Century', p. 26.

introduce more elaborate forms of their performance. As James McKinnon noted, 'Monasticism made a quantitive contribution to the song of the fourth-century church, and received in exchange the gift of musicality.'[28] However, the defence that had to be mounted by certain patristic writers with regard to these innovations suggests that at first not everyone welcomed them.[29]

A second factor that especially helped to develop in the West the notion that *all* the psalms could be sung as the praise of God was the responsibility given to communities of monks from the early fifth century onwards for maintaining the prayer and sacramental life of basilicas in the city of Rome. Even though the external *form* of their daily offices of psalmody may have remained unchanged, yet in this new context their *function* was effectively transformed from the spiritual advancement of the individual members of the community to the celebration of the praise of the Church. Moreover, this Roman institution provided a model that was imitated by others, including the establishment by the Franks of similar foundations in connection with sanctuaries dedicated to specially venerated saints.[30]

What of the difficulty, however, that not all of the psalms actually expressed words of praise to God – indeed that some of them were prayers of desperation and others called down fire upon the psalmist's enemies? This did not present a serious obstacle to the new understanding, because it was thought that it was the *act* of psalm-singing rather than what the *text* of the psalms themselves said that was pleasing to God: we chant the psalms because God likes to hear them. One can see this attitude emerging in the *Rule of the Master*, a forerunner of the *Rule of Benedict* that was written in the late fifth or early sixth century:

> So great must be the reverential seriousness and the manner of chanting the psalms that the Lord listens more lovingly than we say them; as Scripture declares: 'You take delight in the coming of the morning, and in the evening', and again: 'Sing the psalms to him joyfully and skillfully, for direct is the word of the Lord', and again: 'Exult in him with fear', and again: 'Sing to the Lord wisely'. Therefore if it commands the singing of psalms to be done wisely and with fear, the person singing them should stand with body motionless and head bowed, and should sing praises to the Lord with composure, since he is indeed performing his service before the Godhead,

---

[28] McKinnon, 'Desert Monasticism and the Later Fourth-Century Psalmodic Movement', p. 519.

[29] See especially Basil, *Epistula* 207.3; and Niceta of Remesiana, *De psalmodiae bono* 2.

[30] See Angelus Häussling, *Mönchskonvent und Eucharistiefeier*, Liturgiewissenschaftliche Quellen und Forschungen 58 (Aschendorff, Münster 1973), pp. 123–42.

as the prophet teaches when he says: 'In the presence of the angels I will sing your praise'.

So the singer of psalms must always be careful not to let his attention wander elsewhere, lest God say to us when our mind has strayed to some other thought: 'This people honors me only with lip-service, while their hearts are far from me', and lest it likewise be said of us: 'With their mouth they blessed and in their heart they cursed', and lest when we praise God with the tongue alone, we admit God only to the doorway of our mouth while we bring in and lodge the devil in the dwelling of our heart.[31]

It is true that this chapter of the rule, like other sources of the period, later goes on to offer a second and more traditionally monastic reason why the singer should pay attention to every single verse of the psalm, 'because if each verse is noted the soul derives profit for salvation and therein finds all it seeks, for "the psalm says everything for edification"; as the prophet declares: "I shall sing and understand in the way of integrity, when you come to me".'[32] Yet it is clear from the rest of the chapter that praise has succeeded edification as the primary purpose for the use of psalms, and that what makes the psalm acceptable to God as praise is not the words that are spoken but the attitude and intention of the singer.

As a result of this change of function, it was inevitable that less importance would be accorded to the silent prayer that came between the psalms. The *Rule of the Master* (chapter 48) directed that these periods of silence should always be kept short, to avoid the risk of any of the community falling asleep or being tempted to evil thoughts. The *Rule of Benedict* echoed all the above exhortations, although expressing them more succinctly and giving as the reason for brevity in prayer that 'we are not to imagine that our prayers will be heard because we use many words'.[33]

In the light of all this, it is not surprising to find that the period of silence between psalms eventually disappeared altogether in later Western usage, and that the usual method of psalm-singing itself changed. Already by the late fourth century, in an effort to relieve the monotony of the responsorial method, especially during the long night vigils, a variation had emerged – antiphonal psalmody – in which the assembly was divided into two choirs that took it in turns to sing the response to the verses sung by the soloist, or sometimes by two soloists alternating the

---

[31] *Regula Magistri* 47; ET from Luke Eberle, *The Rule of the Master* (Cistercian Publications, Kalamazoo, MI 1977), pp. 205–6.

[32] On the importance attached in the developing monastic tradition to conforming the heart to the words being sung, see Dyer, 'The Psalms in Monastic Prayer', pp. 62–4.

[33] *Rule of Benedict* 19–20. See also Adalbert de Vogüé, *The Rule of St. Benedict: A Doctrinal and Spiritual Commentary* (Cistercian Publications, Kalamazoo, MI 1983), pp. 139–49.

verses.[34] By the ninth century, however, the two choirs themselves, instead of a soloist, began to sing the verses alternately, and the response (or antiphon, as it came to be called) was relegated merely to the beginning and end of the psalm. Joseph Dyer has argued that this change came about as a result of an increasing emphasis on the efficacy of individual effort towards growth in grace. 'Prayers and good works which were frequently repeated added to the soul's store of grace and helped overcome uncertainty about personal salvation. From this perspective active participation in chanting the sacred words of the psalms would have seemed more meritorious than merely listening to them.'[35] While there may certainly be some truth to his claim, such an attitude required as its prerequisite that the act of psalm-singing already be thought of as directed towards God rather than towards the edification of oneself or others.

Psalmody as penance

The use of certain psalms in order to express contrition for one's sins is clearly attested from the fourth century onwards, apparently originating in the strongly penitential atmosphere of urban monastic circles, where Psalm 51 ('Have mercy on me, O God . . .') begins to make an appearance at or near the beginning of each day's worship in several sources. Other appropriate psalms, too, were to be used by individuals in order to ask for the forgiveness of their sins.[36] In addition to this use of particular psalms, we find encouragement for individuals to think of the daily offices as a whole as being an opportunity to acknowledge their faults privately and ask for forgiveness. It is to be noted, however, that there is no evidence to suggest that at this time the rites themselves included any explicitly penitential prayers or litanies. It was only much later that these emerged.[37]

Yet such an attitude towards the offices laid the foundations for the subsequent development of the idea that the act of singing or saying psalms could function as an expression of penitence. Thus Caesarius of Arles in the sixth century lists psalmody among the pious exercises in which a penitent person might engage: 'I believe that in the mercy of God he will deign to inspire you in such a way that you do not pursue sinfulness through neglect, but rather through repentance are able to

---

[34] See Taft, *The Liturgy of the Hours in East and West*, p. 139; idem, 'Christian Liturgical Psalmody', pp. 19–23.

[35] Joseph Dyer, 'Monastic Psalmody of the Middle Ages', *Revue bénédictine* 99 (1989), pp. 41–74, here at pp. 70–1.

[36] See, for example, Athanasius, *Epistula ad Marcellinum* 21.

[37] For further details of all these developments, see below, pp. 135–41.

reach the remedy of forgiveness by fasting, prayer, singing the psalms, and almsgiving.'[38] Similarly, he includes it along with fasting, prayer, and the keeping of vigils as an appropriate Lenten practice.[39]

From this use, psalms then found their way into more formal penitential discipline. The Celtic penitential system, which often assigned the performance of extremely demanding penances for many sins, also permitted commutation – the substitution of an easier or shorter penance for a more arduous or lengthier one. Hence the recitation of a certain number of psalms frequently became the permitted – and much preferred – alternative to other forms of penitential practice. A very early example of this development appears in the so-called *Canones hibernenses*, where as a substitute for a *superpositio* (a double fast-day) 100 psalms may be recited instead.[40] Other Celtic sources regularly speak of multiples of 50 psalms functioning in this manner.

Psalmody as intercession

The roots of the use of psalms for intercessory purposes seem to lie in the funeral customs of the early Church. A notable characteristic of early Christian practice was the singing of psalms and hymns that proclaimed the hope of the resurrection, as death approached, as the body was prepared for burial, and in procession to the grave. One of the most common texts used for this purpose was Psalm 116. This custom stood in sharp contrast to the usual pagan practice of the period, which was to accompany death and burial by wailing and lamentation.[41] As the centuries went by, however, Christianity was increasingly influenced by the surrounding culture, and the fear of judgement and condemnation began to displace confident hope of the resurrection in the liturgies surrounding death. As a result, funeral psalmody took on a more penitential tone, as those present began to recite on behalf of the dying and deceased the sort of psalms that they believed that those persons themselves would have said as prayers for the forgiveness of their sins, had they been able to do so.

---

[38] Caesarius, *Sermones* 208; ET from M. M. Mueller, *Saint Caesarius of Arles – Sermons*, 3, Fathers of the Church 66 (Catholic University of America Press, Washington, DC 1973), p. 89.

[39] *Sermones* 202, 238; ET ibid., pp. 68, 224.

[40] Text in F. W. H. Wasserschleben, *Die Bussordnungen der abendländischen Kirche* (Verlag Graeger, Halle 1851), p. 139. Cyrille Vogel, 'Composition légale et commutations dans le système de la pénitence tarifée', *Revue de droit canonique* 9 (1959), pp. 1–38, here at p. 3, dates this section of the document to the sixth century.

[41] See Geoffrey Rowell, *The Liturgy of Christian Burial*, Alcuin Club Collections 59 (SPCK, London 1977), pp. 19–30.

Our earliest testimony to this development appears to be a document dating from the second half of the eighth century, which describes the monastic observances of Monte Cassino. This states that on the day of the burial of a monk, the community were to chant the seven penitential psalms after vespers.[42] Later sources reveal further developments from this practice: the psalms used were no longer restricted to those that were penitential in character, and the act of intercession could now be for the living as well as the departed. Thus various documents prescribe 50, 100, or the whole 150 psalms to be said on the occasion of a death, and monthly or annually thereafter.[43] Similarly, the biography of Benedict of Aniane (*d.* 821) recounts that he directed that the monks of his monastery, on going to their places in the choir each morning, should recite privately 15 psalms before the office began. These were arranged in three sets of five, the first set being for the living, the second for all the faithful departed, and the third for all the recently deceased. Each set was concluded with a short collect related to the intention for which the preceding psalms had been said. Although the biographer does not specify which particular psalms were used for this purpose, scholars are generally agreed, because of the evidence from later sources, that they were the 15 gradual psalms (Psalms 120–34).[44]

Conclusions

What emerges from this survey is that an important distinction has to be drawn between the first three ways of using the psalms described above and the second three. In the first group, it is the *content* of the psalms that is all-important. It is because of what the psalms say, that they can be used as prophecy, as teaching, or as hymns. While the roots of the second group may lie in this same area, in their later development content recedes into the background, and it is the *action* of singing the psalm and the particular *intention* of the singer that renders it a vehicle for praise, for penitence, or for intercession. One might go so far as to say that in this second group of uses, psalms have simply become the accepted currency for divine–human interchange: their value lay not in their intrinsic merit but solely in the fact that God was thought to favour them. God could just as easily have preferred the performance of some

---

[42] See Edmund Bishop, 'The Prymer', in idem, *Liturgica Historica* (Clarendon Press, Oxford 1918), p. 216.

[43] For examples, see ibid., p. 216, and esp. n. 4.

[44] Ibid., p. 214; Joseph Jungmann, *Christian Prayer through the Centuries* (Paulist Press, New York, 2nd edn, 2007), pp. 53–4.

other form of religious activity, but because he apparently liked to hear psalms, he could in that way be paid what was due to him in praise, be repaid what was owed to him in penitence, or be induced to grant the desires of the supplicants.

The use of content-related psalmody did not of course thereafter vanish from the Christian liturgical tradition. Appropriate psalms and sections of psalms went on being appointed for a wide variety of occasions in the ecclesiastical calendar, and certain psalms continued to be regarded as especially suitable to express particular sentiments. Yet there was now an underlying sense that one psalm was really just as good as another, and that what the words of a text said mattered less than the intentions of those using it. These attitudes have lingered on down to the present day, and often contribute to a lack of sensitivity on the part of those responsible for deciding what psalms shall be used in worship and how they are to be performed, as well as to the confusion of those who are expected to participate in that psalmody.

9

The emergence of penitential prayer

'How can we who died to sin still live in it?', asks Paul in his letter to the Romans (6.2). But some of them did, and in the churches that he founded Paul quickly developed a procedure for dealing with those who committed what was regarded as serious sin after they had been baptized. In 1 Corinthians 5 he instructs the community to assemble with the presence of his spirit and deliver a man who had been living with his father's wife 'to Satan for the destruction of the flesh, that his spirit may be saved in the day of the Lord Jesus' (1 Corinthians 5.5). And he warns them to separate themselves from Christians who are guilty of immorality or greed, or were idolaters, revilers, drunkards or robbers (1 Corinthians 5.11), just as elsewhere he had commanded his readers to keep away from any believers living in idleness (2 Thessalonians 3.6, 14). It appears that it was out of this practice that the penitential disciplines of early Christianity developed.[1]

What, however, of less serious sin in the Christian community, of the kind that did not warrant such drastic measures? Here we know rather less about what went on in the first few centuries. Some early Christian writers in their comments on penitence and conversion appear only to have in mind pre-baptismal sin, and make no reference to failings after baptism. Others appear to refer solely to the post-baptismal sins that require episcopal intervention and the imposition of penitential disciplines and do not acknowledge the persistence of lesser faults among the members of the Church, while still other writings are ambiguous with regard to the object of their remarks: though they may be treating of the daily imperfections of the baptized, it is not obvious that this is so, and hence their evidence is not helpful to the building up of a picture of the existence of penitential prayer within early Christian congregations. Nor is it a subject which many other scholars have studied in any detail, and so here we shall be entering relatively uncharted waters.

---

[1] For the development of what came to be known as the sacrament of penance, see James Dallen, *The Reconciling Community: The Rite of Penance* (Pueblo, New York 1986); Joseph A. Favazza, *The Order of Penitents: Historical Roots and Pastoral Future* (The Liturgical Press, Collegeville 1988).

Earliest signs

Some scattered references do exist among the earliest of Christian writings. There are a few New Testament texts that speak of prayer being made on behalf of those sinning, principally 1 John 5.16 ('If anyone sees his brother committing what is not a mortal sin, he will ask, and God will give him life for those whose sin is not mortal') and James 5.16 ('confess your sins to one another, and pray for one another, that you may be healed'). There are two references in the *Didache* to the confession of sin in the assembly prior to prayer and the celebration of the eucharist (4.14; 14.1), but these are unique in early Christian literature.[2] And there is mention in *1 Clement* of seeking forgiveness for sins that have been committed. Here the context is the expulsion of their leaders from office by some in the Corinthian church, and the author is writing from the church at Rome, apparently around AD 96, and appealing for those involved to acknowledge their wrongdoing rather than harden their hearts.

> The Lord, brothers, is in need of nothing. He desires nothing of any one, except that confession be made to him. For, says the chosen one David, 'I will confess to the Lord; and it will please him more than a young bullock which has horns and hoofs. Let the poor see it, and be glad' [Psalm 69.30–2]. And again he says, 'Sacrifice to God a sacrifice of praise, and pay your vows to the Most High. And call upon me in the day of your trouble, and I will deliver you, and you shall glorify me' [Psalm 50.14–15]. For 'the sacrifice of God is a broken spirit' [Psalm 51.17]. (*1 Clement* 52)

The quotation of the verse from Psalm 51 is interesting here in view of its later prominence in Christian daily prayer. Although apparently by another author and from a different and presumably somewhat later context, the document known as *2 Clement* also calls upon Christians to practise repentance (see, e.g., 8, 13, 16–17).

The third century

When we reach third-century Christian authors, references to penitential prayer become a little more plentiful, and appear in the various treatises

---

[2] On these references, see Aaron Milavec, 'The Purifying Confession of Failings Required by the Didache's Eucharistic Sacrifice', *Biblical Theology Bulletin* 33 (2003), pp. 64–76; Jonathan A. Draper, 'Pure Sacrifice in Didache 14 as Jewish Christian Exegesis', *Neotestamentica* 42 (2008), pp. 223–52; and Carsten Claussen, 'Repentance and Prayer in the *Didache*', in Mark J. Boda, Daniel K. Falk, and Rodney A. Werline (eds), *Seeking the Favor of God*, vol. 3: *The Impact of Penitential Prayer beyond Second Temple Judaism* (Society of Biblical Literature, Atlanta 2008), pp. 197–212.

on prayer that have survived from this period. Thus, Tertullian, writing in North Africa at the beginning of the century and working through the clauses of the Lord's Prayer in his treatise *De oratione*, refers briefly to the clause 'forgive us our sins', and appears to imply – though does not explicitly state – that his readers should engage in regular prayer for pardon, especially as he expected the Lord's Prayer to be recited whenever a person prayed (7; 10). In his treatise *De paenitentia* he enlarges upon the subject of penitence, but only in relation to the possibility of the remission of serious post-baptismal sin through the discipline of penance, and does not mention prayer for forgiveness of other sins. There is, however, a further interesting passage in his treatise on prayer, where he is discussing whether one should stand or kneel to pray. He asks: 'Who would hesitate every day to prostrate himself before God, at least in the first prayer with which we enter on the daylight?' (*De oratione* 23.3). This seems to suggest that it was customary, in his region at least, to begin each morning's prayer with some form of expression of penitence that required kneeling as its accompaniment.

In the similar treatise written by Cyprian of Carthage around half a century later, the author more obviously suggests that regular penitential prayer is needed. 'How necessarily, how providently and salutarily, are we admonished that we are sinners, we who are compelled to supplicate for our sins, so that while pardon is sought from God, the soul examine its conscience! Lest any one should flatter himself that he is innocent, and by exalting himself should more deeply perish, he is instructed and taught that he sins daily while he is told to pray daily for his sins' (*De Dominica oratione* 22).

Such practices do not appear to have been confined to North Africa. In the anonymous Syrian church order known as the *Didascalia Apostolorum*, the author, having asserted that there is no one without sin, is primarily concerned with those who have committed serious sins that require episcopal intervention, but suggests in an allusion to the Lord's Prayer that all Christians need regularly to pray for pardon: 'And again he taught us that we should be constantly praying at all times and saying, "Forgive us our debts, as we also have forgiven our debtors"' (7). The theologian Origen, in his treatise on prayer, insists that kneeling is the necessary posture when praying for forgiveness (*De oratione* 31.3), and that penitence is one of four topics that ought to feature regularly in everyone's prayer – following praise and thanksgiving and before intercession: 'After thanksgiving it seems to me that he ought to blame himself bitterly before God for his own sins and then ask, first for healing that he may be delivered from the habit that brings him to

sin and, second, for forgiveness of the sins that have been committed'
(ibid., 33.1).[3]

Fourth-century daily prayer

In the light of these earlier references, we would naturally expect that among
the more extensive writings on prayer and liturgical practice that survive
from the fourth century the theme of penitence would be much more pro-
minent, especially in the changed circumstances in which Christianity
then found itself, with many new adherents lacking the same high degree
of ethical motivation and testing that had marked earlier converts.[4] But
this is not quite the case.

On the one hand, the need for a penitential aspect to daily prayer is
strongly stressed by a number of Christian authors of the period. John
Chrysostom provides an excellent example of this when he dwells on it
at some length in his instructions to candidates for baptism written
around 390:

> And I urge you to show great zeal by gathering here in the church at dawn
> to make your prayers and confessions to the God of all things, and to thank
> him for the gifts he has already given. Beseech him to deign to lend you
> from now on his powerful aid in guarding this treasure; strengthened with
> this aid, let each one leave the church to take up his daily tasks . . . How-
> ever, let each one approach his daily task with fear and anguish, and spend
> his working hours in the knowledge that at evening he should return here
> to the church, render an account to the Master of his whole day, and beg
> forgiveness for his faults. For even if we are on guard ten thousand times
> a day, we cannot avoid making ourselves accountable for many different
> faults. Either we say something at the wrong time, or we listen to idle talk,
> or we think indecent thoughts, or we fail to control our eyes, or we spend
> time in vain and idle things that have no connection with what we should
> be doing. This is the reason why each evening we must beg pardon from
> the Master for all these faults. This is why we must flee to the loving-
> kindness of God and make our appeal to him.[5]

On the other hand, this penitential tone does not appear to be reflected
in the actual contents of the daily 'cathedral' services in which ordinary
Christians took part. Nearly all accounts of the forms that morning and

---

[3] ET from *Origen*, translation and introduction by Rowan A. Greer (Paulist Press, New York
1979), p. 169.

[4] See Michel Dujarier, *A History of the Catechumenate: The First Six Centuries* (Sadlier, New
York 1979), pp. 78–111.

[5] *Baptismal Instructions* 8.17–18; ET from Harkins, *St John Chrysostom: Baptismal Instructions*,
pp. 126–7.

evening prayer then took lack any reference to the occurrence of an expression of penitence within them, and instead imply that they focused exclusively on praise and intercession. Thus, for example, Eusebius of Caesarea, writing in the first half of the fourth century and our first witness to the now public celebration of the morning and evening times of prayer, speaks of 'hymns, praises, and truly divine delights' being offered to God at those hours, and implies that Psalm 141 was used regularly in the evening (*Commentarius in psalmum* 64.10) and elsewhere that Psalm 63 was its counterpart in the morning (*Commentarius in psalmum* 142.8); the pilgrimage diary kept by Egeria of her visit to Jerusalem in the 380s mentions only that psalms and hymns and intercessions were used in the daily services there (*Itinerarium* 24) but describes them as being always 'suitable, appropriate, and relevant' to the hour of their celebration (ibid. 25.5); and a Syrian church order from the same period, *Apostolic Constitutions*, fleshes out the contents a little more fully, stating explicitly that Psalm 63 was used each morning and Psalm 141 each evening, and providing full texts of the intercessory prayers for those services (2.59; 8.35–9).

John Chrysostom admitted that Psalm 141, which he said was sung every day, was appropriate to the evening, but claimed:

> Not for this reason, however, did the fathers choose this psalm, but rather they ordered it to be said as a salutary medicine and forgiveness of sins, so that whatever has dirtied us throughout the whole length of the day, either in the marketplace or at home or wherever we spend our time, we get rid of it in the evening through this spiritual song. For it is indeed a medicine that destroys all those things.
>
> The morning psalm is of the same sort . . . For it kindles the desire for God, and arouses the soul and greatly inflames it, and fills it with great goodness and love . . . Where there is love of God, all evil departs; where there is remembrance of God there is oblivion of sin and destruction of evil.[6]

It does not seem likely that this explanation for the choice of these psalms is historically accurate. Psalm 141 is a plea not to be tempted to commit sin, rather than a confession of sins already committed. Had the intention been to articulate the latter, more suitable psalms exist that could have been selected, but this is one of the very few that refer to evening. Similarly, the Septuagint translation of Psalm 63 referred to 'early' in its first verse and to 'in the mornings' in verse 6, which would have made it seem suitable for the morning. Hence Chrysostom's interpretation looks very much like reading his own spirituality into the rite.

---

[6] John Chrysostom, *Expositio in psalmum* 140.1; ET from Taft, *The Liturgy of the Hours in East and West*, pp. 42–3.

Of course, the absence of any explicit reference in the various descriptions cannot of itself be considered as conclusive evidence that penitence had not yet made its way into the rites, as these sources tend to be rather brief and do not purport to give every detail – none of them, for instance, explicitly mentions the use of the psalms of praise, 148–50, which scholars generally believe formed the core of daily morning prayer throughout most if not all the ancient Christian world[7] – and so it is conceivable that some penitential prayer did exist in them but was simply not mentioned. However, the reconstructions that have been made by scholars of the oldest strata of some later liturgical texts do lend support to the supposition that there were no penitential elements at the time.[8] Only in Cappadocia is there evidence for the use of the penitential Psalm 51 at the beginning of each day; and the significance of that anomaly will be considered a little later.

Monastic influence

What then are we to make of the apparent discrepancy between the penitential disposition towards daily prayer recommended by Christian authors and the seeming almost total absence of the expression of penitence in the early liturgical rites themselves? The answer appears to lie in the ascetic and monastic movements that developed in the Egyptian and Syrian deserts in the early part of the fourth century. As we saw earlier,[9] their existence became one of almost ceaseless prayer, broken only by the briefest of intervals for sleep and food. While the content of the meditation on which their praying was based was the recitation of all 150 canonical psalms, in their biblical order, psalm alternating with prayer all day long, yet their prayer itself was suffused with a strongly penitential character as they wrestled against the temptations and power of evil.

This same outlook towards prayer seems to have continued even when the desert ascetics formed themselves into monastic communities there. Thus, for example, the *Regulations* of Horsiesios, when speaking about the daily morning and evening assemblies in which this same alternation of reading and prayer occurred, included this counsel for the moments of prayer: 'Then once we are prostrate on our face, let us weep in our hearts for our sins' (8). This attitude was also adopted by the many pious individuals and small groups of ascetics who remained in the cities but wanted

---

[7] See Taft, *The Liturgy of the Hours in East and West*, pp. 191–209.

[8] See, for example, Gabriele Winkler's reconstruction of the ancient Armenian evening office in her essay, 'Über die Kathedralvesper in der verschieden Riten des Ostens und Westens', *Archiv für Liturgiewissenschaft* 16 (1974), pp. 53–102, here at pp. 78–80.

[9] Chapter 7 above, pp. 108–13.

something more demanding for their daily diet than mere attendance at morning and evening prayer with other Christians. What the bishops to whom they turned for guidance recommended to them was the observance of the full round of hours of daily prayer that had been the common practice of ordinary Christians in the third century, but was falling into neglect in the changed circumstances of the fourth. Because many of these bishops had either spent time as monks in the desert themselves or had been influenced by the spirituality of that tradition, it was very likely they who encouraged a more penitential approach towards daily prayer among all Christians (just as we saw in the case of John Chrysostom above, who had lived under the tutelage of a monk earlier in his life), and incorporated it into the rules of life that they drew up for the pious.

Thus, Basil of Caesarea in his *Longer Rules* counsels that at the end of the day at evening prayer not only should thanksgiving be offered for what the worshippers have received during the day or for what they have done rightly, but also 'confession made of what we have failed to do – an offence committed, be it voluntary or involuntary, or perhaps unnoticed, either in word or deed or in the very heart – propitiating God in our prayers for all our failings . . .'.[10]

An even more pronounced penitential tone suffuses the directions about prayer in the anonymous Greek treatise *De virginitate*, once attributed to Athanasius but now thought to be of Cappadocian origin and dating from around AD 370, which directs its readers to pray at the traditional hours of the day (in the morning, at the third, sixth, and ninth hours, in the evening and in the middle of the night) though adding to that pattern a vigil between midnight prayer and morning prayer. At the sixth hour the virgin is told to

> make your prayers with psalms, weeping and petition, because at this hour the Son of God hung on the cross. At the ninth hour again in hymns and praises, confessing your sins with tears, supplicate God, because at that hour the Lord hanging on the cross gave up the spirit.
>
> (Pseudo-Athanasius, *De virginitate* 12)

Similarly, for the prayer in the middle of the night and the vigil of psalmody that followed it, she is instructed:

> first say this verse: 'At midnight I rose to praise you because of your righteous ordinances' [Ps. 119.62], and pray and begin to say the fiftieth psalm [i.e., Psalm 51] until you complete it, and let these things remain fixed for

---

[10] Basil, *Regulae fusius tractatae* 37.4; ET from Taft, *The Liturgy of the Hours in East and West*, p. 86.

you every day. Say as many psalms as you can say standing, and after each psalm let there be a prayer and genuflection, confessing your sins with tears to the Lord and asking him to forgive you . . .'   (ibid., 20)

It is interesting to observe the use of Psalm 51 at what was for this group of female ascetics the beginning of their day, immediately after they had said their midnight prayer. This seems to be a continuation of the practice described by Tertullian of kneeling for 'the first prayer with which we enter on the daylight' mentioned above. It is not surprising to find this tradition, which had once been intended for ordinary Christians, being preserved only within this urban monastic setting, However, whether the use of Psalm 51 itself went back to Tertullian's day or whether the tradition known to him of beginning each morning's praying with a penitential prayer of some sort stabilized only at a later date into this particular psalm is impossible to know.

It is true that one other fourth-century source records Psalm 51 as forming the beginning of morning prayer, but that is also of Cappadocian origin, a letter written by Basil about the same time as the *De virginitate*. He describes a vigil service which begins with penitence ('among us the people go at night to the house of prayer, and, in distress, affliction, and continual tears making confession to God, at last rise from their prayers and begin to sing psalms') and concludes at dawn, when they 'all together, as with one voice and one heart, raise the psalm of confession to the Lord, each forming for himself his own expressions of penitence'.[11] The mention of 'the people' might seem to suggest that Basil is describing the practice of ordinary Christians here. However, it is very probable that these particular people were for the most part the especially devout: it is unlikely that many of the average churchgoers of this period would have regularly spent a night in corporate prayer, especially as Chrysostom complains that his congregations could not be persuaded even to engage in the traditional hours of prayer at the third, sixth, and ninth hours or to study the Bible at home.[12] This suggests that Psalm 51 may after all not have been a customary part of normal 'cathedral' usage but had been introduced under the influence of ascetics.

Support is lent by some other sources to the supposition that it was a later addition. John Cassian in an account of the monastic prayer he had experienced in Bethlehem describes how in his own day (the 380s) an extra morning service had been added to the traditional daily round so that the monks should not go back to bed for too long after they had

---

[11] Basil, *Epistula* 207.3–4; ET from *NPNF*, Second Series, 8:247.
[12] See John Chrysostom, *De Anna sermo* 4.5; *Homiliae in Matthaeum* 2.5.

finished the nightly vigil and the original morning office (which centred round Psalms 148–50) but instead get up again for this service, which, he says, consisted of Psalms 51, 63, and 90.[13] These psalms thus appear to have been imported as secondary elements from other regions where they were already associated in some way with the morning and were not part of the indigenous tradition. Similarly, John Chrysostom does not seem to have been familiar with the regular use of Psalm 51 in the mornings at Antioch. Not only does he not mention it explicitly, in spite of his emphasis on the penitential dimension of daily prayer, but when he is describing the pattern of prayer followed by monastic groups there, he refers to Psalms 148–150 as forming the conclusion of the nightly vigil, and says that after a short period of rest, 'as soon as the sun is up, or rather even long before its rise, [they] rise up from their bed . . . and having made one choir . . . with one voice all, like as out of one mouth, they sing hymns unto the God of all, honouring him and thanking him for all his benefits . . .'.[14] This seems to indicate that this service began immediately with praise rather than penitence.[15]

Cassian even adds that 'throughout Italy' Psalm 51 came after Psalms 148–50 each morning[16] and not before them as one might have expected. Robert Taft believes he must be mistaken here,[17] but if Cassian were accurately recording the practice, then that sequence too might imply that Psalm 51 was at first a secondary appendage to the rite and only subsequently found its place at the very beginning of the service.

Later developments

It is only later that we see signs of a somewhat pronounced penitential dimension in the rites of morning and evening prayer more generally, apparently as the influence of monastic spirituality took greater hold. Thus, eventually Psalm 51 tended to be inserted at the beginning of the morning office throughout the ancient Christian world, although some exceptions seem to have persisted. In southern Gaul in the monastic rules of Caesarius of Arles and his successor Aurelian in the sixth century it still came at the beginning of nocturns, as it had done in *De virginitate*; and the Council of Barcelona (*c*.540) directed that it was to be said 'before the canticle' at

---

[13] John Cassian, *De institutis coenobiorum* 3.4–6.
[14] John Chrysostom, *Homiliae in Matthaeum* 68.3; ET from *NPNF*, First Series, 10:400.
[15] Pace Taft, *The Liturgy of the Hours in East and West*, pp. 82–3.
[16] John Cassian, *De institutis coenobiorum* 3.6.
[17] Taft, *The Liturgy of the Hours in East and West*, p. 128.

the morning office (canon 1) – the need for such a direction being a sure sign that its use was still not yet universal in Spain.[18]

A penitential element was eventually also added to the evening office, especially in the East. Before the end of the fourth century the morning and evening services had come to be understood as the spiritual counterpart and fulfilment of the morning and evening sacrifices of the first covenant (see, for example, John Chrysostom, *Expositio in psalmum* 140.3), and from the fifth century onwards a literal offering of incense began to make an appearance in some regional rites in accordance with Exodus 30.7–8.[19] While the offering of incense in the morning offices was generally interpreted as symbolizing the prayers of the saints rising to God, as it is in Revelation 8.3–4, in the evening it came to be thought of in a number of traditions as an expiatory oblation for the sins of the people, as in Numbers 16.46–7, and attracted to itself substantial penitential material.[20]

Penitential days?

Even though, to begin with, penitential prayer does not seem to have featured much in the ordinary daily services of the 'cathedral' tradition, what about those particular days that were set apart in the annual calendar for fasting? Were they also days of penitential prayer? As early as the *Didache*, Christians were instructed to observe every Wednesday and Friday as fast days, so that they would not be like 'the hypocrites' (i.e., the Jews) who fasted on Mondays and Thursdays (8.1). Opinion has been divided as to whether these days were chosen by Jewish Christians simply to distinguish themselves from other Jews or whether this was already a variant Jewish tradition, perhaps linked to the solar calendar of the Essenes.[21] The same pattern is also mentioned in some other early Christian sources, indicating that it was not just a peculiarity of the tradition behind the *Didache*, but was more widely practised.[22] The various references to it, however, do not imply that it had a particularly penitential character. Among Latin authors, the days were known as *stationes*, times of being 'on sentry duty'

---

[18] Ibid., pp. 107, 158.

[19] The earliest explicit reference seems to be Theodoret, Bishop of Cyrrhus in Syria, *Quaestiones in Exodum* 28, written sometime after AD 453.

[20] For further details, see Gabriele Winkler, 'L'aspect pénitentiel dans les offices du soir en Orient et en Occident', in *Liturgie et rémission des péchés: conférences Saint Serge XXe Semaine d'Études Liturgiques*, Bibliotheca Ephemerides Liturgicae Subsidia 3 (Edizioni Liturgiche, Rome 1975), pp. 273–93.

[21] See for example Annie Jaubert, 'Jésus et le calendrier de Qumran', *New Testament Studies* 7 (1960), pp. 1–30; Willy Rordorf, *Sunday* (SCM Press, London 1968), pp. 183–6.

[22] Clement of Alexandria, *Stromata* 7.12; Origen, *Homiliae in Leviticum* 10.2; *Didascalia* 21.

or 'on watch', suggesting eschatological vigilance rather than penitence as such.[23] Although special services came to be held on those days, usually services of the word at the ninth hour, being the end of the normal working day after which the fast would be broken and the main meal of the day consumed, these do not seem to have contained any specially penitential elements as far as we can judge from the limited evidence available.[24]

As for the season of Lent, one of the oldest extant references to a period of forty days does concern those who were undergoing penitential discipline, but the emphasis both in this case and in other early sources falls upon the commemoration and symbolic sharing in Jesus' forty-day fast in the wilderness and upon resisting temptation rather than contrition for sins.[25] Although some may argue that fasting necessarily always involved some element of penitence, yet once again this is not a note that receives any particular emphasis in the early Lenten liturgical rites themselves, as far as we know them.

The eucharist

Perhaps the most surprising discovery of all is that penitential prayers appear to be almost completely lacking from early eucharistic rites. Although our very ancient source, the *Didache*, referred to above, seemed to have implied the need for confession of sins within the assembly prior to a celebration of that rite, reference to such a custom is not found again in this connection. Any indication of a penitential note is absent from the description of eucharistic practice given by Justin Martyr in the middle of the second century (*First Apology* 65–7), although that might be accounted for by the fact that his account was intended for a pagan audience and so would not necessarily have included every detail of the rite. But it is also absent from all other references to the eucharist, until the Lord's Prayer, with its petition for forgiveness, makes its first appearance in some, but apparently not all, eucharistic rites in the second half of the fourth century, being placed after the eucharistic prayer and before communion.[26]

---

[23] *Shepherd of Hermas*, Similitude 5.1; Tertullian, *De oratione* 19; *De ieiunio* 10; 14.

[24] See Bradshaw, *Daily Prayer in the Early Church*, pp. 91–2.

[25] See Maxwell E. Johnson, 'Preparation for Pascha? Lent in Christian Antiquity', in Paul F. Bradshaw and Lawrence A. Hoffman (eds), *Passover and Easter: The Symbolic Structuring of Sacred Seasons* (University of Notre Dame Press, Notre Dame 1999), pp. 36–54, here at pp. 44ff.

[26] In the *Mystagogical Catecheses* attributed to Cyril of Jerusalem (5.11); apparently alluded to by Ambrose of Milan (*De sacramentis* 5.24); and at Antioch according to John Chrysostom: see F. van de Paverd, 'Anaphoral Intercessions, Epiclesis and Communion Rites in John Chrysostom', *Orientalia Christiana Periodica* 49 (1983), pp. 303–39.

Robert Taft has suggested that the reason for the addition of that prayer to the eucharist at this time was precisely in order to introduce a petition for forgiveness into the liturgy in association with the new notes of fear and awe that were beginning to be attached to the eucharist in the course of the fourth century.[27] But a sense of unworthiness to receive the eucharist had been prevalent among Christians since much earlier in the century and had led many to abstain from communion for long periods of time – in some cases as much as a year or more.[28] Why then was penitence so slow to find a place within eucharistic celebrations, and why, when it did, was it such a limited expression as a line in the Lord's Prayer?

It seems most improbable that Christians regularly practised some form of confession or penitential prayer before or within their eucharistic celebration throughout this long period but somehow no one ever mentioned it in their writings about the eucharist. Yet, given the various references to the need to ask for forgiveness for one's sins found in early Christian writers, it seems odd that it was so late in emerging in connection with this central rite. Could it have something to do with the ancient tradition of celebrating the eucharist only on Sundays? There was a general prohibition from both fasting and kneeling for prayer on that day of the week.[29] If kneeling was thus forbidden, that meant that penitential prayer could not be offered. It is interesting to observe that ancient forms of morning prayer that begin with Psalm 51 on weekdays generally do not do so on Sundays. It is usually replaced on that day by the canticle *Benedicite* (Daniel 3.35–68), a song of creation especially appropriate to the first day of the week.[30] This would seem to support the hypothesis that Sunday was considered an inappropriate day for penitential prayer. As a result, the absence of any opportunity for confession and absolution before receiving communion, unless one entered upon the rigorous process of canonical penance intended for truly serious sins, may well account for the prolonged abstinence from communion that we encounter being so often adopted at this period. And if lay people were commonly not receiving communion, that in turn may account also for the continuing lack of penitential prayers within eucharistic rites for several centuries afterwards, even when the eucharist was celebrated on weekdays.

Thus, although brief penitential notes are occasionally sounded in some eucharistic prayers that may go back at least in part to the fourth

[27] Taft, 'The Lord's Prayer in the Eucharistic Liturgy: When and Why?', p. 153.

[28] See, for example, John Chrysostom, *Homiliae in epistulam ad Hebraeos* 17.7; Ambrose, *De sacramentis* 5.25; and for discussion of the reasons for such abstentions, see above, pp. 34–5.

[29] For the earliest references to this rule, see Tertullian, *De corona* 3; *De oratione* 23.

[30] Taft, *The Liturgy of the Hours in East and West*, p. 89.

century (for example, a petition for forgiveness of sins in the Anaphora of Addai and Mari, a reference to the worshippers as being 'sinners and unworthy and wretched' in the Egyptian version of the Anaphora of Basil, and a similar reference to 'us sinners' in the Roman Canon of the Mass),[31] penitential prayers proper do not appear in the texts of eucharistic rites until the ninth or tenth centuries in either East or West. These, however, were merely the formalization of an older tradition of informal preparatory prayers that clergy and other communicants had engaged in for some centuries prior to this, and are found both at the very beginning of the rite and immediately prior to the reception of communion.[32] Because laity now made their communion infrequently, they did not need to be involved in these devotions on a regular basis, and, on those few occasions when they did receive communion, especially in the West, they were increasingly expected to make their confession and receive absolution well beforehand each time, as well as undertaking a prior period of fasting or abstinence. Later still, however, pre-communion devotions for the laity of a penitential kind were introduced into the rite itself.[33]

Conclusion

Thus, there appears to have been a dichotomy between the counsel offered by many Christian leaders and spiritual writers in the early centuries of Christianity and its emerging liturgical traditions. While the former strongly advocated within every individual an awareness of sin that needed frequent confession, the rites themselves focused almost exclusively on praise and intercession. It was only very gradually, initially apparently through the increasing influence of monasticism on liturgy, that some expression of penitence began to appear both in the daily services and in the eucharist. It is small wonder, therefore, that in modern rites there is uncertainty as to whether every act of worship should always include such an element, and if so, where in the rite it should be located.

---

[31] For ET of these prayers, see R. C. D. Jasper and G. J. Cuming, *Prayers of the Eucharist: Early and Reformed* (Collins, London 1975), pp. 28, 31, 108.

[32] See further Robert F. Taft, 'Byzantine Communion Rites II: Later Formulas and Rubrics in the Ritual of Clergy Communion', *Orientalia Christiana Periodica* 67 (2001), pp. 275–352; Annewies van den Hoek and Stefanos Alexopoulos, 'The Endicott Scroll and its Place in the History of Private Communion Prayers', *Dumbarton Oaks Papers* 60 (2006), pp. 145–88; Joseph A. Jungmann, *The Mass of the Roman Rite* (Benzinger, New York 1951), I, pp. 290–311; II, pp. 343–50.

[33] Jungmann, *The Mass of the Roman Rite*, II, pp. 363–4, 367–74.

Index of Modern Authors

References to pages which provide full bibliographical details are indicated by the use of **boldface** type.

Index of Names and Subjects